Return

to

Naples

Jacques Casanova de Seingalt

[ZHINGOORA BOOKS]

RETURN TO NAPLES

ROME—NAPLES—BOLOGNA

CHAPTER VIII

Cardinal Passianei—The Pope—Masiuccia—I Arrive At Naples

Cardinal Passionei received me in a large hall where he was writing. He begged me to wait till he had finished, but he could not ask me to take a seat as he occupied the only chair that his vast room contained.

When he had put down his pen, he rose, came to me, and after informing me that he would tell the Holy Father of my visit, he added,—

"My brother Cornaro might have made a better choice, as he knows the Pope does not like me."

"He thought it better to choose the man who is esteemed than the man who is merely liked."

"I don't know whether the Pope esteems me, but I am sure he knows I don't esteem him. I both liked and esteemed him before he was pope, and I concurred in his election, but since he has worn the tiara it's a different matter; he has shewn himself too much of a 'coglione'."

"The conclave ought to have chosen your eminence."

"No, no; I'm a root-and-branch reformer, and my hand would not have been stayed for fear of the vengeance of the guilty, and God alone knows what would have come of that. The only cardinal fit to be pope was Tamburini; but it can't be helped now. I hear people coming; good-bye, come again to-morrow."

What a delightful thing to have heard a cardinal call the Pope a fool, and name Tamburini as a fit person. I did not lose a moment in noting this pleasant circumstance down: it was too precious a morsel to let slip. But who was Tamburini? I had never heard of him. I asked Winckelmann, who dined with me.

"He's a man deserving of respect for his virtues, his character, his firmness, and his farseeing intelligence. He has never disguised his opinion of the Jesuits, whom he styles the fathers of deceits, intrigues, and lies; and that's what made Passionei mention him. I think, with him, that Tamburini would be a great and good pope."

I will here note down what I heard at Rome nine years later from the mouth of a tool of the Jesuits. The Cardinal Tamburini was at the last gasp, and the conversation turned upon him, when somebody else said,—

"This Benedictine cardinal is an impious fellow after all; he is on his death-bed, and he has asked for the viaticum, without wishing to purify his soul by confession."

I did not make any remark, but feeling as if I should like to know the truth of the matter I asked somebody about it next day, my informant being a person who must have known the truth, and could not have had any motive for disguising the real facts of the case. He told me that the cardinal had said mass three days before,

4

and that if he had not asked for a confessor it was doubtless because he had nothing to confess.

Unfortunate are they that love the truth, and do not seek it out at its source. I hope the reader will pardon this digression, which is not without interest.

Next day I went to see Cardinal Passionei, who told me I was quite right to come early, as he wanted to learn all about my escape from The Leads, of which he had heard some wonderful tales told.

"I shall be delighted to satisfy your eminence, but the story is a long one."

"All the better; they say you tell it well."

"But, my lord, am I to sit down on the floor?"

"No, no; your dress is too good for that."

He rang his bell, and having told one of his gentlemen to send up a seat, a servant brought in a stool. A seat without a back and without arms! It made me quite angry. I cut my story short, told it badly, and had finished in a quarter of an hour.

"I write better than you speak," said he.

"My lord, I never speak well except when I am at my ease."

"But you are not afraid of me?"

"No, my lord, a true man and a philosopher can never make me afraid; but this stool of yours . . . ."

"You like to be at your ease, above all things."

"Take this, it is the funeral oration of Prince Eugene; I make you a present of it. I hope you will approve of my Latinity. You can kiss the Pope's feet tomorrow at ten o'clock."

When I got home, as I reflected on the character of this strange cardinal—a wit, haughty, vain, and boastful, I resolved to make him a fine present. It was the 'Pandectarum liber unicus' which M. de F. had given me at Berne, and which I did not know what to do with. It was a folio well printed on fine paper, choicely bound, and in perfect preservation. As chief librarian the present should be a valuable one to him, all the more as he had a large private library, of which my friend the Abbe Winckelmann was librarian. I therefore wrote a short Latin letter, which I enclosed in another to Winckelmann, whom I begged to present my offering to his eminence.

I thought it was as valuable as his funeral oration at any rate, and I hoped that he would give me a more comfortable chair for the future.

Next morning, at the time appointed, I went to Monte Cavallo, which ought to be called Monte Cavalli, as it gets its name from two fine statues of horses standing on a pedestal in the midst of the square, where the Holy Father's palace is situated.

I had no real need of being presented to the Pope by anyone, as any Christian is at liberty to go in when he sees the door open. Besides I had known His Holiness when he was Bishop of Padua;

but I had preferred to claim the honor of being introduced by a cardinal.

After saluting the Head of the Faithful, and kissing the holy cross embroidered on his holy slipper, the Pope put his right hand on my left shoulder, and said he remembered that I always forsook the assembly at Padua, when he intoned the Rosary.

"Holy Father, I have much worse sins than that on my conscience, so I come prostrate at your foot to receive your absolution."

He then gave me his benediction, and asked me very graciously what he could do for me.

"I beg Your Holiness to plead for me, that I may be able to return to Venice."

"We will speak of it to the ambassador, and then we will speak again to you on the matter."

"Do you often go and see Cardinal Passionei?"

"I have been three times. He gave me his funeral oration on Prince Eugene, and in return I sent him the 'Pandects'."

"Has he accepted them?"

"I think so, Holy Father."

"If he has, he will send Winckelmann to pay you for them."

"That would be treating me like a bookseller; I will not receive any payment."

"Then he will return the volume of the 'Pandects'; we are sure of it, he always does so."

"If his eminence returns me the 'Pandects', I will return him his funeral oration."

At this the Pope laughed till his sides shook.

"We shall be pleased to hear the end of the story without anyone being informed of our innocent curiosity."

With these words, a long benediction delivered with much unction informed me that my audience was at an end.

As I was leaving His Holiness's palace, I was accosted by an old abbe, who asked me respectfully if I were not the M. Casanova who had escaped from The Leads.

"Yes," said I, "I am the man."

"Heaven be praised, worthy sir, that I see you again in such good estate!"

"But whom have I the honour of addressing?"

"Don't you recollect me? I am Momolo, formerly gondolier at Venice."

"Have you entered holy orders, then?"

"Not at all, but here everyone wears the cassock. I am the first scopatore (sweeper) of His Holiness the Pope."

"I congratulate you on your appointment, but you mustn't mind me laughing."

"Laugh as much as you like. My wife and daughters laugh when I put on the cassock and bands, and I laugh myself, but here the dress gains one respect. Come and see us."

"Where do you live?"

"Behind the Trinity of Monti; here's my address."

"I will come to-night."

I went home delighted with this meeting, and determined to enjoy the evening with my Venetian boatman. I got my brother to come with me, and I told him how the Pope had received me.

The Abbe Winckelmann came in the afternoon and informed me that I was fortunate enough to be high in favour with his cardinal, and that the book I had sent him was very valuable; it was a rare work, and in much better condition than the Vatican copy.

"I am commissioned to pay you for it."

"I have told his eminence that it was a present."

"He never accepts books as presents, and he wants yours for his own library; and as he is librarian of the Vatican Library he is afraid lest people might say unpleasant things."

"That's very well, but I am not a bookseller; and as this book only cost me the trouble of accepting it, I am determined only to sell it at the same price. Pray ask the cardinal to honour me by accepting it."

"He is sure to send it back to you."

"He can if he likes, but I will send back his funeral oration, as I am not going to be under an obligation to anyone who refuses to take a present from me."

Next morning the eccentric cardinal returned me my Pandects, and I immediately returned his funeral oration, with a letter in which I pronounced it a masterpiece of composition, though I laid barely glanced over it in reality. My brother told me I was wrong, but I did not trouble what he said, not caring to guide myself by his rulings.

In the evening my brother and I went to the 'scopatore santissimo', who was expecting me, and had announced me to his family as a prodigy of a man. I introduced my brother, and proceeded to a close scrutiny of the family. I saw an elderly woman, four girls, of whom the eldest was twenty-four, two small boys, and above all universal ugliness. It was not inviting for a man of voluptuous tastes, but I was there, and the best thing was to put a good face on it; so I stayed and enjoyed myself. Besides the general ugliness, the household presented the picture of misery, for the 'scopatore santissimo' and his numerous family were obliged to live on two hundred Roman crowns a year, and as there are no perquisites attached to the office of apostolic sweeper, he was compelled to furnish all needs out of this slender sum. In spite of that Momolo was a most generous man. As soon as he saw me seated he told me he should have liked to give me a good supper, but there was only pork chops and a polenta.

"They are very nice," said I; "but will you allow me to send for half a dozen flasks of Orvieto from my lodging?"

"You are master here."

I wrote a note to Costa, telling him to bring the six flasks directly, with a cooked ham. He came in half an hour, and the four girls cried when they saw him, "What a fine fellow!" I saw Costa was delighted with this reception, and said to Momolo,

"If you like him as well as your girls I will let him stay."

Costa was charmed with such honour being shewn him, and after thanking me went into the kitchen to help the mother with the polenta.

The large table was covered with a clean cloth, and soon after they brought in two huge dishes of polenta and an enormous pan full of chops. We were just going to begin when a knocking on the street door was heard.

"'Tis Signora Maria and her mother," said one of the boys.

At this announcement I saw the four girls pulling a wry face. "Who asked them?" said one. "What do they want?" said another. "What troublesome people they are!" said a third. "They might have stayed at home," said the fourth. But the good, kindly father said, "My children, they are hungry, and they shall share what Providence has given us."

I was deeply touched with the worthy man's kindness. I saw that true Christian charity is more often to be found in the breasts of the poor than the rich, who are so well provided for that they cannot feel for the wants of others.

While I was making these wholesome reflections the two hungry ones came in. One was a young woman of a modest and pleasant aspect, and the other her mother, who seemed very humble and as if ashamed of their poverty. The daughter saluted the company with that natural grace which is a gift of nature, apologizing in some confusion for her presence, and saying that she would not have taken the liberty to come if she had known there was company. The worthy Momolo was the only one who answered her, and he said, kindly, that she had done quite right to come, and put her a chair between my brother and myself. I looked at her and thought her a perfect beauty.

Then the eating began and there was no more talking. The polenta was excellent, the chops delicious, and the ham perfect, and in less than an hour the board was as bare as if there had been nothing on it; but the Orvieto kept the company in good spirits. They began to talk of the lottery which was to be drawn the day after next, and all the girls mentioned the numbers on which they had risked a few bajocchi.

"If I could be sure of one number," said I, "I would stake something on it."

Mariuccia told me that if I wanted a number she could give me one. I laughed at this offer, but in the gravest way she named me the number 27.

"Is the lottery still open?" I asked the Abbe Momolo.

"Till midnight," he replied, "and if you like I will go and get the number for you."

"Here are fifty crowns," said I, "put twenty-five crowns on 27-this for these five young ladies; and the other twenty-five on 27 coming out the fifth number, and this I will keep for myself."

He went out directly and returned with the two tickets.

My pretty neighbour thanked me and said she was sure of winning, but that she did not think I should succeed as it was not probable that 27 would come out fifth.

"I am sure of it," I answered, "for you are the fifth young lady I saw in this house." This made everybody laugh. Momolo's wife told me I would have done much better if I had given the money to the poor, but her husband told her to be quiet, as she did not know my intent. My brother laughed, and told me I had done a foolish thing. "I do, sometimes," said I, "but we shall see how it turns out, and when one plays one is obliged either to win or lose."

I managed to squeeze my fair neighbour's hand, and she returned the pressure with all her strength. From that time I knew that my fate with Mariuccia was sealed. I left them at midnight, begging the worthy Momolo to ask me again in two days' time, that we might rejoice together over our gains. On our way home my brother said I had either become as rich as Croesus or had gone mad. I told him that both suppositions were incorrect, but that Mariuccia was as handsome as an angel, and he agreed.

Next day Mengs returned to Rome, and I supped with him and his family. He had an exceedingly ugly sister, who for all that, was a good and talented woman. She had fallen deeply in love with my brother, and it was easy to see that the flame was not yet extinguished, but whenever she spoke to him, which she did whenever she could get an opportunity, he looked another way.

She was an exquisite painter of miniatures, and a capital hand at catching a likeness. To the best of my belief she is still living at Rome with Maroni her husband. She often used to speak of my brother to me, and one day she said that he must be the most thankless of men or he would not despise her so. I was not curious enough to enquire what claim she had to his gratitude.

Mengs's wife was a good and pretty woman, attentive to her household duties and very submissive to her husband, though she could not have loved him, for he was anything but amiable. He was obstinate and fierce in his manner, and when he dined at home he made a point of not leaving the table before he was drunk; out of his own house he was temperate to the extent of not drinking anything but water. His wife carried her obedience so far as to serve as his model for all the nude figures he painted. I spoke to her one day about this unpleasant obligation, and she said that her confessor had charged her to fulfil it, "for," said he, "if your husband has another woman for a model he will be sure to enjoy her before painting her, and that sin would be laid to your charge."

After supper, Winckelmann, who was as far gone as all the other male guests, played with Mengs's children. There was nothing of the pedant about this philosopher; he loved children and young people, and his cheerful disposition made him delight in all kinds of enjoyment.

Next day, as I was going to pay my court to the Pope, I saw Momolo in the first ante-chamber, and I took care to remind him of the polenta for the evening.

As soon as the Pope saw me, he said,—

"The Venetian ambassador has informed us that if you wish to return to your native land, you must go and present yourself before the secretary of the Tribunal."

"Most Holy Father, I am quite ready to take this step, if Your Holiness will grant me a letter of commendation written with your own hand. Without this powerful protection I should never dream of exposing myself to the risk of being again shut up in a place from which I escaped by a miracle and the help of the Almighty."

"You are gaily dressed; you do not look as if you were going to church."

"True, most Holy Father, but neither am I going to a ball."

"We have heard all about the presents being sent back. Confess that you did so to gratify your pride."

"Yes, but also to lower a pride greater than mine."

The Pope smiled at this reply, and I knelt down and begged him to permit me to present the volume of Pandects to the Vatican Library. By way of reply he gave me his blessing, which signifies, in papal language, "Rise; your request is granted."

"We will send you," said he, "a mark of our singular affection for you without your having to pay any fees."

A second blessing bid me begone. I have often felt what a good thing it would be if this kind of dismissal could be employed in general society to send away importunate petitioners, to whom one does not dare say, "Begone."

I was extremely curious to know what the Pope had meant by "a mark of our singular affection." I was afraid that it would be a blessed rosary, with which I should not have known what to do.

When I got home I sent the book by Costa to the Vatican, and then I went to dine with Mengs. While we were eating the soup the winning numbers from the lottery were brought in. My brother glanced at them and looked at me with astonishment. I was not thinking of the subject at that moment, and his gaze surprised me.

"Twenty-seven," he cried, "came out fifth."

"All the better," said I, "we shall have some amusement out of it."

I told the story to Mengs, who said,—

"It's a lucky folly for you this time; but it always is a folly."

He was quite right, and I told him that I agreed with him; but I added that to make a worthy use of the fifteen hundred roman crowns which fortune had given me, I should go and spend fifteen days at Naples.

"I will come too," said the Abbe Alfani. "I will pass for your secretary."

"With all my heart," I answered, "I shall keep you to your word."

I asked Winckelmann to come and eat polenta with the scopatore santissimo, and told my brother to shew him the way; and I then called on the Marquis Belloni, my banker, to look into my accounts, and to get a letter of credit on the firm at Naples, who were his agents. I still had two hundred thousand francs: I had jewellery worth thirty thousand francs, and fifty thousand florins at Amsterdam.

I got to Momolo's in the dusk of the evening, and I found Winckelmann and my brother already there; but instead of mirth reigning round the board I saw sad faces on all sides.

"What's the matter with the girls?" I asked Momolo.

"They are vexed that you did not stake for them in the same way as you did for yourself."

"People are never satisfied. If I had staked for them as I did for myself, and the number had come out first instead of fifth, they would have got nothing, and they would have been vexed then. Two days ago they had nothing, and now that they have twenty-seven pounds apiece they ought to be contented."

"That's just what I tell them, but all women are the same."

"And men too, dear countryman, unless they are philosophers. Gold does not spell happiness, and mirth can only be found in hearts devoid of care. Let us say no more about it, but be happy."

Costa placed a basket containing ten packets of sweets, upon the table.

"I will distribute them," said I, "when everybody is here."

On this, Momolo's second daughter told me that Mariuccia and her mother were not coming, but that they would send them the sweets.

"Why are they not coming?"

"They had a quarrel yesterday," said the father, "and Mariuccia, who was in the right, went away saying that she would never come here again."

"You ungrateful girls!" said I, to my host's daughters, "don't you know that it is to her that you owe your winnings, for she gave me the number twenty-seven, which I should never have thought of. Quick! think of some way to make her come, or I will go away and take all the sweets with me."

"You are quite right," said Momolo.

The mortified girls looked at one another and begged their father to fetch her.

"Ira," said he, "that won't do; you made her say that she would never come here again, and you must make up the quarrel."

They held a short consultation, and then, asking Costa to go with them, they went to fetch her.

In half an hour they returned in triumph, and Costa was quite proud of the part he had taken in the reconciliation. I then distributed the sweets, taking care to give the two best packets to the fair Mary.

A noble polenta was placed upon the board, flanked by two large dishes of pork chops. But Momolo, who knew my tastes, and whom I had made rich in the person of his daughters, added to the feast some delicate dishes and some excellent wine. Mariuccia was simply dressed, but her elegance and beauty and the modesty of her demeanour completely seduced me.

We could only express our mutual flames by squeezing each other's hands; and she did this so feelingly that I could not doubt her love. As we were going out I took care to go downstairs beside her and asked if I could not meet her by herself, to which she replied by making an appointment with me for the next day at eight o'clock at the Trinity of Monti.

Mariuccia was tall and shapely, a perfect picture, as fair as a white rose, and calculated to inspire voluptuous desires. She had beautiful light brown hair, dark blue eyes, and exquisitely arched eyelids. Her mouth, the vermilion of her lips, and her ivory teeth were all perfect. Her well-shaped forehead gave her an air approaching the majestic. Kindness and gaiety sparkled in her eyes; while her plump white hands, her rounded finger-tips, her pink nails, her breast, which the corset seemed scarcely able to restrain, her dainty feet, and her prominent hips, made her worthy of the chisel of Praxiteles. She was just on her eighteenth year, and so far had escaped the connoisseurs. By a lucky chance I came across her in a poor and wretched street, and I was fortunate enough to insure her happiness.

It may easily be believed that I did not fail to keep the appointment, and when she was sure I had seen her she went out of the church. I followed her at a considerable distance: she entered a ruined building, and I after her. She climbed a flight of steps which seemed to be built in air, and when she had reached the top she turned.

"No one will come and look for me here," said she, "so we can talk freely together."

I sat beside her on a stone, and I then declared my passionate love for her.

"Tell me," I added, "what I can do to make you happy; for I wish to possess you, but first to shew my deserts."

"Make me happy, and I will yield to your desires, for I love you."

"Tell me what I can do."

"You can draw me out of the poverty and misery which overwhelm me. I live with my mother, who is a good woman, but devout to the point of superstition; she will damn my soul in her efforts to save it. She finds fault with my keeping myself clean, because I have to touch myself when I wash, and that might give rise to evil desires.

"If you had given me the money you made me win in the lottery as a simple alms she would have made me refuse it, because you might have had intentions. She allows me to go by myself to mass because our confessor told her she might do so; but I dare not stay away a minute beyond the time, except on feast days, when I am allowed to pray in the church for two or three hours. We can only meet here, but if you wish to soften my lot in life you can do so as follows:

"A fine young man, who is a hairdresser, and bears an excellent character, saw me at Momolo's a fortnight ago, and met me at the church door next day and gave me a letter. He declared himself my lover, and said that if I could bring him a dowry of four hundred crowns, he could open a shop, furnish it, and marry me.

"'I am poor,' I answered, 'and I have only a hundred crowns in charity tickets, which my confessor keeps for me.' Now I have two hundred crowns, for if I marry, my mother will willingly give me her share of the money you made us gain. You can therefore make me happy by getting me tickets to the amount of two hundred crowns more. Take the tickets to my confessor, who is a very good man and fond of me; he will not say anything to my mother about it."

"I needn't go about seeking for charity tickets, my angel. I will take two hundred piastres to your confessor to-morrow, and you must manage the rest yourself. Tell me his name, and to-morrow I will tell you what I have done, but not here, as the wind and the cold would be the death of me. You can leave me to find out a room where we shall be at our ease, and without any danger of people suspecting that we have spent an hour together. I will meet you at the church to-morrow at the same hour and when you see me follow me."

Mariuccia told me her confessor's name, and allowed me all the caresses possible in our uncomfortable position. The kisses she gave me in return for mine left no doubt in my mind, as to her love for me. As nine o'clock struck I left her, perishing with cold, but burning with desire; my only thought being where to find a room in which I might possess myself of the treasure the next day.

On leaving the ruined palace, instead of returning to the Piazza di Spagna I turned to the left and passed along a narrow and dirty street only inhabited by people of the lowest sort. As I slowly walked along, a woman came out of her house and asked me politely if I were looking for anybody.

"I am looking for a room to let."

"There are none here, sir, but, you will find a hundred in the square."

"I know it, but I want the room to be here, not for the sake of the expense, but that I may be sure of being able to spend an hour or so of a morning with a person in whom I am interested. I am ready to pay anything."

"I understand what you mean, and you should have a room in my house if I had one to spare, but a neighbour of mine has one on the ground floor, and if you will wait a moment I will go and speak to her."

"You will oblige me very much."

"Kindly step in here."

I entered a poor room, where all seemed wretchedness, and I saw two children doing their lessons. Soon after, the good woman came back and asked me to follow her. I took several pieces of money from my pocket, and put them down on the only table which this poor place contained. I must have seemed very generous, for the poor mother came and kissed my hand with the utmost gratitude. So pleasant is it to do good, that now when I have nothing left the remembrance of the happiness I have given to others at small cost is almost the only pleasure I enjoy.

I went to a neighbouring house where a woman received me in an empty room, which she told me she would let cheaply if I would pay three months in advance, and bring in my own furniture.

"What do you ask for the three months' rent?"

"Three Roman crowns."

"If you will see to the furnishing of the room this very day I will give you twelve crowns."

"Twelve crowns! What furniture do you want?"

"A good clean bed, a small table covered with a clean cloth, four good chairs, and a large brazier with plenty of fire in it, for I am nearly perishing of cold here. I shall only come occasionally in the morning, and I shall leave by noon at the latest."

"Come at three o'clock, then, to-day, and you will find everything to your satisfaction."

From there I went to the confessor. He was a French monk, about sixty, a fine and benevolent-looking man, who won one's respect and confidence.

"Reverend father," I began, "I saw at the house of Abbe Momolo, 'scoptore santissimo', a young girl named Mary, whose confessor you are. I fell in love with her, and offered her money to try and seduce her. She replied that instead of trying to lead her into sin I would do better to get her some charity tickets that she might be able to marry a young man who loved her, and would make her happy. I was touched by what she said, but my passion still remained. I spoke to her again, and said that I would give her two hundred crowns for nothing, and that her mother should keep them.

"'That would be my ruin,' said she; 'my mother would think the money was the price of sin, and would not accept it. If you are really going to be so generous, take the money to my confessor, and ask him to do what he can for my marriage.'"

"Here, then, reverend father, is the sum of money for the good girl; be kind enough to take charge of it, and I will trouble her no more.

I am going to Naples the day after to-morrow, and I hope when I come back she will be married."

The good confessor took the hundred sequins and gave me a receipt, telling me that in interesting myself on behalf of Mariuccia I was making happy a most pure and innocent dove, whom he had confessed since she was five years old, and that he had often told her that she might communicate without making her confession because he knew she was incapable of mortal sin.

"Her mother," he added, "is a sainted woman, and as soon as I have enquired into the character of the future husband I will soon bring the marriage about. No one shall ever know from whom this generous gift comes."

After putting this matter in order I dined with the Chevalier Mengs, and I willingly consented to go with the whole family to the Aliberti Theatre that evening. I did not forget, however, to go and inspect the room I had taken. I found all my orders executed, and I gave twelve crowns to the landlady and took the key, telling her to light the fire at seven every morning.

So impatient did I feel for the next day to come that I thought the opera detestable, and the night for me was a sleepless one.

Next morning I went to the church before the time, and when Mariuccia came, feeling sure that she had seen me, I went out. She followed me at a distance, and when I got to the door of the lodging I turned for her to be sure that it was I, and then went in and found the room well warmed. Soon after Mariuccia came in, looking timid, confused, and as if she were doubtful of the path she was treading. I clasped her to my arms, and reassured her by my tender embraces; and her courage rose when I shewed her the confessor's receipt, and told her that the worthy man had promised to care for her marriage. She kissed my hand in a transport of delight, assuring me that she would never forget my kindness. Then, as I urged her to make me a happy man, she said,—

"We have three hours before us, as I told my mother I was going to give thanks to God for having made me a winner in the lottery."

This reassured me, and I took my time, undressing her by degrees, and unveiling her charms one by one, to my delight, without the slightest attempt at resistance on her part. All the time she kept her eyes fixed on mine, as if to soothe her modesty; but when I beheld and felt all her charms I was in an ecstasy. What a body; what beauties! Nowhere was there the slightest imperfection. She was like Venus rising from the foam of the sea. I carried her gently to the bed, and while she strove to hide her alabaster breasts and the soft hair which marked the entrance to the sanctuary, I undressed in haste, and consummated the sweetest of sacrifices, without there being the slightest doubt in my mind of the purity of the victim. In the first sacrifice no doubt the young priestess felt some pain, but she assured me out of delicacy that she had not been hurt, and at the second assault she shewed that she shared my flames. I was going to immolate the victim for the third time when the clock struck ten. She began to be restless, and hurriedly put on our clothes. I had to go to Naples, but I assured her that the desire of embracing her once more before her marriage would hasten my return to Rome. I promised to take another hundred crowns to her confessor, advising her to spend the money she had won in the lottery on her trousseau.

"I shall be at Monolo's to-night, dearest, and you must come, too; but we must appear indifferent to each other, though our hearts be full of joy, lest those malicious girls suspect our mutual understanding."

"It is all the more necessary to be cautious," she replied, "as I have noticed that they suspect that we love each other."

Before we parted she thanked me for what I had done for her, and begged me to believe that, her poverty notwithstanding, she had given herself for love alone.

I was the last to leave the house, and I told my landlady that I should be away for ten or twelve days. I then went to the confessor to give him the hundred crowns I had promised my mistress. When the good old Frenchman heard that I had made this fresh sacrifice that Mariuccia might be able to spend her lottery winnings on her clothes, he told me that he would call on the mother that very day and urge her to consent to her daughter's marriage, and also learn where the young man lived. On my return from Naples I heard that he had faithfully carried out his promise.

I was sitting at table with Mengs when a chamberlain of the Holy Father called. When he came in he asked M. Mengs if I lived there, and on that gentleman pointing me out, he gave me, from his holy master, the Cross of the Order of the Golden Spur with the diploma, and a patent under the pontifical seal, which, in my quality as doctor of laws, made me a prothonotary-apostolic 'extra urbem'.

I felt that I had been highly honoured, and told the bearer that I would go and thank my new sovereign and ask his blessing the next day. The Chevalier Mengs embraced me as a brother, but I had the advantage over him in not being obliged to pay anything, whereas the great artist had to disburse twenty-five Roman crowns to have his diploma made out. There is a saying at Rome, 'Sine efusione sanguinis non fit remissio', which may be interpreted, Nothing without money; and as a matter of fact, one can do anything with money in the Holy City.

Feeling highly flattered at the favour the Holy Father had shewn me, I put on the cross which depended from a broad red ribbon-red being the colour worn by the Knights of St. John of the Lateran, the companions of the palace, 'comites palatini', or count-palatins. About the same time poor Cahusac, author of the opera of Zoroaster, went mad for joy on the receipt of the same order. I was not so bad as that, but I confess, to my shame, that I was so proud of my decoration that I asked Winckelmann whether I should be allowed to have the cross set with diamonds and rubies. He said I could if I liked, and if I wanted such a cross he could get me one cheap. I was delighted, and bought it to make a show at Naples, but I had not the face to wear it in Rome. When I went to thank the Pope I wore the cross in my button-hole out of modesty. Five years afterwards when I was at Warsaw, Czartoryski, a Russian prince-palatine, made me leave it off by saying,—

"What are you doing with that wretched bauble? It's a drug in the market, and no one but an impostor would wear it now."

The Popes knew this quite well, but they continued to give the cross to ambassadors while they also gave it to their 'valets de chambre'. One has to wink at a good many things in Rome.

In the evening Momolo gave me a supper by way of celebrating my new dignity. I recouped him for the expense by holding a bank at faro, at which I was dexterous enough to lose forty crowns to the family, without having the slightest partiality to Mariuccia who won like the rest. She found the opportunity to tell me that her confessor had called on her, that she had told him where her future husband lived, and that the worthy monk had obtained her mother's consent to the hundred crowns being spent on her trousseau.

I noticed that Momolo's second daughter had taken a fancy to Costa, and I told Momolo that I was going to Naples, but that I would leave my man in Rome, and that if I found a marriage had been arranged on my return I would gladly pay the expenses of the wedding.

Costa liked the girl, but he did not marry her then for fear of my claiming the first-fruits. He was a fool of a peculiar kind, though fools of all sorts are common enough. He married her a year later after robbing me, but I shall speak of that again.

Next day, after I had breakfasted and duly embraced my brother, I set out in a nice carriage with the Abbe Alfani, Le Duc preceding me on horseback, and I reached Naples at a time when everybody was in a state of excitement because an eruption of Vesuvius seemed imminent. At the last stage the inn-keeper made me read the will of his father who had died during the eruption of 1754. He said that in the year 1761 God would overwhelm the sinful town of Naples, and the worthy host consequently advised me to return to Rome. Alfani took the thing seriously, and said that we should do well to be warned by so evident an indication of the will of God. The event was predicted, therefore it had to happen. Thus a good many people reason, but as I was not of the number I proceeded on my way.

CHAPTER IX

My Short But Happy Stay at Naples—The Duke de Matalone My Daughter—Donna Lucrezia—My Departure

I shall not, dear reader, attempt the impossible, however much I should like to describe the joy, the happiness, I may say the ecstasy, which I experienced in returning to Naples, of which I had such pleasant memories, and where, eighteen years ago, I had made my first fortune in returning from Mataro. As I had come there for the second time to keep a promise I had made to the Duke de Matalone to come and see him at Naples, I ought to have visited this nobleman at once; but foreseeing that from the time I did so I should have little liberty left me, I began by enquiring after all my old friends.

I walked out early in the morning and called on Belloni's agent. He cashed my letter of credit and gave me as many bank-notes as I liked, promising that nobody should know that we did business together. From the bankers I went to see Antonio Casanova, but they told me he lived near Salerno, on an estate he had bought which gave him the title of marquis. I was vexed, but I had no right to expect to find Naples in the statu quo I left it. Polo was dead, and his son lived at St. Lucia with his wife and children; he was a boy when I saw him last, and though I should have much liked to see him again I had no time to do so.

It may be imagined that I did not forget the advocate, Castelli, husband of my dear Lucrezia, whom I had loved so well at Rome and Tivoli. I longed to see her face once more, and I thought of the joy with which we should recall old times that I could never forget. But Castelli had been dead for some years, and his widow lived at a distance of twenty miles from Naples. I resolved not to return to Rome without embracing her. As to Lelio Caraffa, he was still alive and residing at the Matalone Palace.

I returned, feeling tired with my researches, dressed with care, and drove to the Matalone Palace, where they told me that the duke was at table. I did not care for that but had my name sent in, and the duke came out and did me the honour of embracing me and thouing me, and then presented me to his wife, a daughter of the Duke de Bovino, and to the numerous company at table. I told him I had only come to Naples in fulfillment of the promise I had made him at Paris.

"Then," said he, "you must stay with me;" and, without waiting for my answer, ordered my luggage to be brought from the inn, and my carriage to be placed in his coach-house. I accepted his invitation.

One of the guests, a fine-looking man, on hearing my name announced, said gaily,—

"If you bear my name, you must be one of my father's bastards."

"No," said I, directly, "one of your mother's."

This repartee made everybody laugh, and the gentleman who had addressed me came and embraced me, not in the least offended. The joke was explained to me. His name was Casalnovo, not Casanova, and he was duke and lord of the fief of that name.

"Did you know," said the Duke de Matalone, "that I had a son?"

"I was told so, but did not believe it, but now I must do penance for my incredulity, for I see before me an angel capable of working this miracle."

The duchess blushed, but did not reward my compliment with so much as a glance; but all the company applauded what I had said, as it was notorious that the duke had been impotent before his marriage. The duke sent for his son, I admired him, and told the father that the likeness was perfect. A merry monk, who sat at the right hand of the duchess, said, more truthfully, that there was no likeness at all. He had scarcely uttered the words when the duchess coolly gave him a box on the ear, which the monk received with the best grace imaginable.

I talked away to the best of my ability, and in half an hour's time I had won everybody's good graces, with the exception of the duchess, who remained inflexible. I tried to make her talk for two days without success; so as I did not care much about her I left her to her pride.

As the duke was taking me to my room he noticed my Spaniard, and asked where my secretary was, and when he saw that it was the Abbe Alfani, who had taken the title so as to escape the notice of the Neapolitans, he said,—

"The abbe is very wise, for he has deceived so many people with his false antiques that he might have got into trouble."

He took me to his stables where he had some superb horses, Arabs, English, and Andalusians; and then to his gallery, a very fine one; to his large and choice library; and at last to his study, where he had a fine collection of prohibited books.

I was reading titles and turning over leaves, when the duke said,—

"Promise to keep the most absolute secrecy on what I am going to shew you."

I promised, without making any difficulty, but I expected a surprise of some sort. He then shewed me a satire which I could not understand, but which was meant to turn the whole Court into ridicule. Never was there a secret so easily kept.

"You must come to the St. Charles Theatre," said he, "and I will present you to the handsomest ladies in Naples, and afterwards you can go when you like, as my box is always open to my friends. I will also introduce you to my mistress, and she, I am sure, will always be glad to see you."

"What! you have a mistress, have you?"

"Yes, but only for form's sake, as I am very fond of my wife. All the same, I am supposed to be deeply in love with her, and even jealous, as I never introduce anyone to her, and do not allow her to receive any visitors."

"But does not your young and handsome duchess object to your keeping a mistress?"

"My wife could not possibly be jealous, as she knows that I am impotent—except, of course, with her."

"I see, but it seems strange; can one be said to have a mistress whom one does not love?"

"I did not say I loved her not; on the contrary, I am very fond of her; she has a keen and pleasant wit, but she interests my head rather than my heart."

"I see; but I suppose she is ugly?"

"Ugly? You shall see her to-night, and you can tell me what you think of her afterwards. She is a handsome and well-educated girl of seventeen."

"Can she speak French?"

"As well as a Frenchwoman."

"I am longing to see her."

When we got to the theatre I was introduced to several ladies, but none of them pleased me. The king, a mere boy, sat in his box in the middle of the theatre, surrounded by his courtiers, richly but tastefully dressed. The pit was full and the boxes also. The latter were ornamented with mirrors, and on that occasion were all illuminated for some reason or other. It was a magnificent scene, but all this glitter and light put the stage into the background.

After we had gazed for some time at the scene, which is almost peculiar to Naples, the duke took me to his private box and introduced me to his friends, who consisted of all the wits in the town.

I have often laughed on hearing philosophers declare that the intelligence of a nation is not so much the result of the climate as of education. Such sages should be sent to Naples and then to St. Petersburg, and be told to reflect, or simply to look before them. If the great Boerhaave had lived at Naples he would have learnt more about the nature of sulphur by observing its effects on vegetables, and still more on animals. In Naples, and Naples alone, water, and nothing but water, will cure diseases which are fatal elsewhere, despite the doctors' efforts.

The duke, who had left me to the wits for a short time, returned and took me to the box of his mistress, who was accompanied by an old lady of respectable appearance. As he went in he said, "Leonilda mia, ti presento il cavalier Don Giacomo Casanova, Veneziano, amico mio'."

She received me kindly and modestly, and stopped listening to the music to talk to me.

When a woman is pretty, one recognizes her charms instantaneously; if one has to examine her closely, her beauty is doubtful. Leonilda was strikingly beautiful. I smiled and looked at the duke, who had told me that he loved her like a daughter, and that he only kept her for form's sake. He understood the glance, and said,—

"You may believe me."

"It's credible," I replied.

Leonilda no doubt understood what we meant, and said, with a shy smile,—

"Whatever is possible is credible."

"Quite so," said I, "but one may believe, or not believe, according to the various degrees of possibility."

"I think it's easier to believe than to disbelieve. You came to Naples yesterday; that's true and yet incredible."

"Why incredible?"

"Would any man suppose that a stranger would come to Naples at a time when the inhabitants are wishing themselves away?"

"Indeed, I have felt afraid till this moment, but now I feel quite at my ease, since, you being here, St. Januarius will surely protect Naples."

"Why?"

"Because I am sure he loves you; but you are laughing at me."

"It is such a funny idea. I am afraid that if I had a lover like St. Januarius I should not grant him many favours."

"Is he very ugly, then?"

"If his portrait is a good likeness, you can see for yourself by examining his statue."

Gaiety leads to freedom, and freedom to friendship. Mental graces are superior to bodily charms.

Leonilda's frankness inspired my confidence, and I led the conversation to love, on which she talked like a past mistress.

"Love," said she, "unless it leads to the possession of the beloved object, is a mere torment; if bounds are placed to passion, love must die."

"You are right; and the enjoyment of a beautiful object is not a true pleasure unless it be preceded by love."

"No doubt if love precedes it accompanies, but I do not think it necessarily follows, enjoyment."

"True, it often makes love to cease."

"She is a selfish daughter, then, to kill her father; and if after enjoyment love still continue in the heart of one, it is worse than murder, for the party in which love still survives must needs be wretched."

"You are right; and from your strictly logical arguments I conjecture that you would have the senses kept in subjection: that is too hard!"

"I would have nothing to do with that Platonic affection devoid of love, but I leave you to guess what my maxim would be."

"To love and enjoy; to enjoy and love. Turn and turn about."

"You have hit the mark."

With this Leonilda burst out laughing, and the duke kissed her hand. Her governess, not understanding French, was attending to the opera, but I was in flames.

Leonilda was only seventeen, and was as pretty a girl as the heart could desire.

The duke repeated a lively epigram of Lafontaine's on "Enjoyment," which is only found in the first edition of his works. It begins as follows:—

> "La jouissance et les desirs
> Sont ce que l'homme a de plus rare;
> Mais ce ne sons pas vrais plaisirs
> Des le moment qu'on les separe."

I have translated this epigram into Italian and Latin; in the latter language I was almost able to render Lafontaine line for line; but I had to use twenty lines of Italian to translate the first ten lines of the French. Of course this argues nothing as to the superiority of the one language over the other.

In the best society at Naples one addresses a newcomer in the second person singular as a peculiar mark of distinction. This puts both parties at their ease without diminishing their mutual respect for one another.

Leonilda had already turned my first feeling of admiration into something much warmer, and the opera, which lasted for five hours, seemed over in a moment.

After the two ladies had gone the duke said, "Now we must part, unless you are fond of games of chance."

"I don't object to them when I am to play with good hands."

"Then follow me; ten or twelve of my friends will play faro, and then sit down to a cold collation, but I warn you it is a secret, as gaming is forbidden. I will answer for you keeping your own counsel, however."

"You may do so."

He took me to the Duke de Monte Leone's. We went up to the third floor, passed through a dozen rooms, and at last reached the gamester's chamber. A polite-looking banker, with a bank of about four hundred sequins, had the cards in his hands. The duke introduced me as his friend, and made me sit beside him. I was going to draw out my purse, but I was told that debts were not paid for twenty-four hours after they were due. The banker gave me a pack of cards, with a little basket containing a thousand counters. I told the company that I should consider each counter as a Naples ducat. In less than two hours my basket was empty. I stopped playing and proceeded to enjoy my supper. It was arranged in the Neapolitan style, and consisted of an enormous dish of macaroni and ten or twelve different kinds of shellfish which are plentiful on the Neapolitan coasts. When we left I took care not to give the duke time to condole with me on my loss, but began to talk to him about his delicious Leonilda.

Early next day he sent a page to my room to tell me that if I wanted to come with him and kiss the king's hand I must put on my gala dress. I put on a suit of rose-coloured velvet, with gold spangles, and I had the great honour of kissing a small hand, covered with chilblains, belonging to a boy of nine. The Prince de St. Nicander brought up the young king to the best of his ability, but he was naturally a kindly, just, and generous monarch; if he had had more dignity he would have been an ideal king; but he was too unceremonious, and that, I think, is a defect in one destined to rule others.

I had the honour of sitting next the duchess at dinner, and she deigned to say that she had never seen a finer dress. "That's my way," I said, "of distracting attention from my face and figure." She smiled, and her politeness to me during my stay were almost limited to these few words.

When we left the table the duke took me to the apartment occupied by his uncle, Don Lelio, who recognized me directly. I kissed the venerable old man's hand, and begged him to pardon me for the freaks of my youth. "It's eighteen years ago," said he, "since I chose M. Casanova as the companion of your studies." I delighted him by giving him a brief account of my adventures in Rome with Cardinal Acquaviva. As we went out, he begged me to come and see him often.

Towards the evening the duke said,—

"If you go to the Opera Buffa you will please Leonilda."

He gave me the number of her box, and added,—

"I will come for you towards the close, and we will sup together as before."

I had no need to order my horses to be put in, as there was always a carriage ready for me in the courtyard.

When I got to the theatre the opera had begun. I presented myself to Leonilda, who received me with the pleasant words, "Caro Don Giacomo, I am so pleased to see you again."

No doubt she did not like to thou me, but the expression of her eyes and the tone of her voice were much better than the to which is often used lavishly at Naples.

The seductive features of this charming girl were not altogether unknown to me, but I could not recollect of what woman she reminded me. Leonilda was certainly a beauty, and something superior to a beauty, if possible. She had splendid light chestnut hair, and her black and brilliant eyes, shaded by thick lashes, seemed to hear and speak at the same time. But what ravished me still more was her expression, and the exquisite appropriateness of the gestures with which she accompanied what she was saying. It seemed as if her tongue could not give speech to the thoughts which crowded her brain. She was naturally quick-witted, and her intellect had been developed by an excellent education.

The conversation turned upon Lafontaine's epigram, of which I had only recited the first ten verses, as the rest is too licentious; and she said,—

"But I suppose it is only a poet's fancy, at which one could but smile."

"Possibly, but I did not care to wound your ears."

"You are very good," said she, using the pleasant tu, "but all the same, I am not so thin-skinned, as I have a closet which the duke has had painted over with couples in various amorous attitudes. We go there sometimes, and I assure you that I do not experience the slightest sensation."

"That may be through a defect of temperament, for whenever I see well-painted voluptuous pictures I feel myself on fire. I wonder that while you and the duke look at them, you do not try to put some of them into practice."

"We have only friendship for one another."

"Let him believe it who will."

"I am sure he is a man, but I am unable to say whether he is able to give a woman any real proofs of his love."

"Yet he has a son."

"Yes, he has a child who calls him father; but he himself confesses that he is only able to shew his manly powers with his wife."

"That's all nonsense, for you are made to give birth to amorous desires, and a man who could live with you without being able to possess you ought to cease to live."

"Do you really think so?"

"Dear Leonilda, if I were in the duke's place I would shew you what a man who really loves can do."

"Caro Don Giacomo, I am delighted to hear you love me, but you will soon forget me, as you are leaving Naples."

"Cursed be the gaming-table, for without it we might spend some delightful hour together."

"The duke told me that you lost a thousand ducats yesterday evening like a perfect gentleman. You must be very unlucky."

"Not always, but when I play on a day in which I have fallen in love I am sure to lose."

"You will win back your money this evening."

"This is the declaration day; I shall lose again."

"Then don't play."

"People would say I was afraid, or that all my money was gone."

"I hope at all events that you will win sometimes, and that you will tell me of your good luck. Come and see me to-morrow with the duke."

The duke came in at that moment, and asked me if I had liked the opera.
Leonilda answered for me,

"We have been talking about love all the time, so we don't know what has been going on the stage."

"You have done well."

"I trust you will bring M. Casanova to see me tomorrow morning, as I hope he will bring me news that he has won."

"It's my turn to deal this evening, dearest, but whether he wins or loses you shall see him to-morrow. You must give us some breakfast."

"I shall be delighted."

We kissed her hand, and went to the same place as the night before. The company was waiting for the duke. There were twelve members of the club, and they all held the bank in turn. They said that this made the chances more equal; but I laughed at this opinion, as there is nothing more difficult to establish than equality between players.

The Duke de Matalone sat down, drew out his purse and his pocket-book, and put two thousand ducats in the bank, begging pardon of the others for doubling the usual sum in favour of the stranger. The bank never exceeded a thousand ducats.

"Then," said I, "I will hazard two thousand ducats also and not more, for they say at Venice that a prudent player never risks more than he can win. Each of my counters will be equivalent to two ducats." So saying, I took ten notes of a hundred ducats each from my pocket, and gave them to the last evening's banker who had won them from me.

Play began; and though I was prudent, and only risked my money on a single card, in less than three hours my counters were all gone. I stopped playing, though I had still twenty-five thousand ducats; but I had said that I would not risk more than two thousand, and I was ashamed to go back from my word.

Though I have always felt losing my money, no one has ever seen me put out, my natural gaiety was heightened by art on such occasions, and seemed to be more brilliant than ever. I have always found it a great advantage to be able to lose pleasantly.

I made an excellent supper, and my high spirits furnished me with such a fund of amusing conversation that all the table was in a roar. I even succeeded in dissipating the melancholy of the Duke de Matalone, who was in despair at having won such a sum from his friend and guest. He was afraid he had half ruined me, and also that people might say he had only welcomed me for the sake of my money.

As we returned to the palace the conversation was affectionate on his side and jovial on mine, but I could see he was in some trouble, and guessed what was the matter. He wanted to say that I could pay the money I owed him whenever I liked, but was afraid of wounding my feelings; but as soon as he got in he wrote me a friendly note to the effect that if I wanted money his banker would let me have as much as I required. I replied directly that I felt the generosity of his offer, and if I was in need of funds I would avail myself of it.

Early next morning I went to his room, and after an affectionate embrace I told him not to forget that we were going to breakfast with his fair mistress. We both put on great coats and went to Leonilda's pretty house.

We found her sitting up in bed, negligently but decently dressed, with a dimity corset tied with red ribbons. She looked beautiful, and her graceful posture added to her charms. She was reading Crebillon's Sopha. The duke sat down at the bottom of the bed, and I stood staring at her in speechless admiration, endeavouring to recall to my memory where I had seen such another face as hers. It seemed to me that I had loved a woman like her. This was the first time I had seen her without the deceitful glitter of candles. She laughed at my absent-mindedness, and told me to sit down on a chair by her bedside.

The duke told her that I was quite pleased at having lost two thousand ducats to his bank, as the loss made me sure she loved me.

"Caro mio Don Giacomo, I am sorry to hear that! You would have done better not to play, for I should have loved you all the same, and you would have been two thousand ducats better off."

"And I two thousand ducats worse off," said the duke, laughing.

"Never mind, dear Leonilda, I shall win this evening if you grant me some favour to-day. If you do not do so, I shall lose heart, and you will mourn at my grave before long."

"Think, Leonilda, what you can do for my friend."

"I don't see that I can do anything."

The duke told her to dress, that we might go and breakfast in the painted closet. She began at once, and preserved a just mean in what she let us see and what she concealed, and thus set me in flames, though I was already captivated by her face, her wit, and her charming manners. I cast an indiscreet glance towards her beautiful breast, and thus added fuel to the fire. I confess that I only obtained this satisfaction by a species of larceny, but I could not have succeeded if she had not been well disposed towards me. I pretended to have seen nothing.

While dressing she maintained with much ingenuity that a wise girl will be much more chary of her favours towards a man she loves than towards a man she does not love, because she would be afraid to lose the first, whereas she does not care about the second.

"It will not be so with me, charming Leonilda," said I.

"You make a mistake, I am sure."

The pictures with which the closet where we breakfasted was adorned were admirable more from the colouring and the design than from the amorous combats they represented.

"They don't make any impression on me," said the duke, and he shewed us that it was so.

Leonilda looked away, and I felt shocked, but concealed my feelings.

"I am in the same state as you," said I, "but I will not take the trouble of convincing you."

"That can't be," said he; and passing his hand rapidly over me he assured himself that it was so. "It's astonishing," he cried; "you must be as impotent as I am."

"If I wanted to controvert that assertion one glance into Leonilda's eyes would be enough."

"Look at him, dearest Leonilda, that I may be convinced."

Leonilda looked tenderly at me, and her glance produced the result I had expected.

"Give me your hand," said I, to the poor duke, and he did so.

"I was in the wrong," he exclaimed, but when he endeavoured to bring the surprising object to light I resisted. He persisted in his endeavours, and I determined to play on him a trick. I took Leonilda's hand and pressed my lips to it, and just as the duke thought he had triumphed I besprinkled him, and went off into a roar of laughter. He laughed too, and went to get a napkin.

The girl could see nothing of all this, as it went on under the table; and while my burning lips rested on her hand, my eyes were fixed on hers and our breath mingled. This close contact had enabled me to baptise the duke, but when she took in the joke we made a group worthy of the pen of Aretin.

It was a delightful breakfast, though we passed certain bounds which decency ought to have proscribed to us, but Leonilda was wonderfully innocent considering her position. We ended the scene by mutual embraces, and when I took my burning lips from Leonilda's I felt consumed with a fire which I could not conceal.

When we left I told the duke that I would see his mistress no more, unless he would give her up to me, declaring that I would marry her and give her a dower of five thousand ducats.

"Speak to her, and if she consents I will not oppose it. She herself will tell you what property she has."

I then went to dress for dinner. I found the duchess in the midst of a large circle, and she told me kindly that she was very sorry to hear of my losses.

"Fortune is the most fickle of beings, but I don't complain of my loss—nay, when you speak thus I love it, and I even think that you will make me win this evening."

"I hope so, but I am afraid not; you will have to contend against Monte
Leone, who is usually very lucky."

In considering the matter after dinner, I determined for the future to play with ready money and not on my word of honour, lest I should at any time be carried away by the excitement of play and induced to stake more than I possessed. I thought, too, that the banker might have his doubts after the two heavy losses I had sustained, and I confess that I was also actuated by the gambler's superstition that by making a change of any kind one changes the luck.

I spent four hours at the theatre in Leonilda's box, where I found her more gay and charming than I had seen her before.

"Dear Leonilda," I said, "the love I feel for you will suffer no delay and no rivals, not even the slightest inconstancy. I have told the duke that I am ready to marry you, and that I will give you a dower of five thousand ducats."

"What did he say?"

"That I must ask you, and that he would offer no opposition."

"Then we should leave Naples together."

"Directly, dearest, and thenceforth death alone would part us."

"We will talk of it to-morrow, dear Don Giacomo, and if I can make you happy I am sure you will do the same by me."

As she spoke these delightful words the duke came in.

"Don Giacomo and I are talking of marrying," said she.

"Marriage, mia carissima," he replied, "ought to be well considered beforehand."

"Yes, when one has time; but my dear Giacomo cannot wait, and we shall have plenty of time to think it over afterwards."

"As you are going to marry," said the duke, "you can put off your departure, or return after the wedding."

"I can neither put it off nor return, my dear duke. We have made up our minds, and if we repent we have plenty of time before us."

He laughed and said we would talk it over next day. I gave my future bride a kiss which she returned with ardour, and the duke and I went to the club, where we found the Duke de Monte Leone dealing.

"My lord," said I, "I am unlucky playing on my word of honour, so I hope you will allow me to stake money."

"Just as you please; it comes to the same thing, but don't trouble yourself. I have made a bank of four thousand ducats that you may be able to recoup yourself for your losses."

"Thanks, I promise to break it or to lose as much."

I drew out six thousand ducats, gave two thousand ducats to the Duke de Matalone, and began to punt at a hundred ducats. After a short time the duke left the table, and I finally succeeded in breaking the bank. I went back to the place by myself, and when I told the duke of my victory the next day, he embraced me with tears of joy, and advised me to stake money for the future.

As the Princess de Vale was giving a great supper, there was no play that evening. This was some respite. We called on Leonilda, and putting off talking of our marriage till the day after we spent the time in viewing the wonders of nature around Naples. In the evening I was introduced by a friend at the princess's supper, and saw all the highest nobility of the place.

Next morning the duke told me that he had some business to do, and that I had better go and see Leonilda, and that he would call for me later on. I went to Leonilda, but as the duke did not put in an appearance we could not settle anything about our marriage. I spent several hours with her, but I was obliged to obey her commands, and could only shew myself amorous in words. Before leaving I repeated that it only rested with her to unite our lives by indissoluble ties, and to leave Naples almost immediately.

When I saw the duke he said,—

"Well, Don Giacomo, you have spent all the morning with my mistress; do you still wish to marry her?"

"More than ever; what do you mean?"

"Nothing; and as you have passed this trial to which I purposely subjected you, we will discuss your union tomorrow, and I hope you will make this charming woman happy, for she will be an excellent wife."

"I agree with you."

When we went to Monte Leone's in the evening, we saw a banker with a good deal of gold before him. The duke told me he was Don Marco Ottoboni. He was a fine-looking man, but he held the cards so closely together in his left hand that I could not see them. This did not inspire me with confidence, so I only punted a ducat at a time. I was persistently unlucky, but I only lost a score of ducats.

After five or six deals the banker, asked me politely why I staked such small sums against him.

"Because I can't see half the pack," I replied, "and I am afraid of losing."

Some of the company laughed at my answer.

Next night I broke the bank held by the Prince the Cassaro, a pleasant and rich nobleman, who asked me to give him revenge, and invited me to supper at his pretty house at Posilipo, where he lived with a virtuosa of whom he had become amorous at Palermo. He also invited the Duke de Matalone and three or four other gentlemen. This was the only occasion on which I held the bank while I was at Naples, and I staked six thousand ducats after warning the prince that as it was the eve of my departure I should only play for ready money.

He lost ten thousand ducats, and only rose from the table because he had no more money. Everybody left the room, and I should have done the same if the prince's mistress had not owed me a hundred ducats. I continued to deal in the hope that she would get her money back, but seeing that she still lost I put down the cards, and told her that she must pay me at Rome. She was a handsome and agreeable woman, but she did not inspire me with any passions, no doubt because my mind was occupied with another, otherwise I should have drawn a bill on sight, and paid myself without meddling with her purse. It was two o'clock in the morning when I got to bed.

Both Leonilda and myself wished to see Caserta before leaving Naples, and the duke sent us there in a carriage drawn by six mules, which went faster than most horses. Leonilda's governess accompanied us.

The day after, we settled the particulars of our marriage in a conversation which lasted for two hours.

"Leonilda," began the duke, "has a mother, who lives at a short distance from here, on an income of six hundred ducats, which I have given her for life, in return for an estate belonging to her husband; but Leonilda does not depend on her. She gave her up to me seven years ago, and I have given her an annuity of five hundred ducats, which she will bring to you, with all her diamonds and an extensive trousseau. Her mother gave her up to me entirely, and I gave my word of honour to get her a good husband. I have taken peculiar care of her education, and as her mind has developed I have put her on her guard against all prejudices, with the exception of that which bids a woman keep herself intact for her future husband. You may rest assured that you are the first man whom Leonilda (who is a daughter to me) has pressed to her heart."

I begged the duke to get the contract ready, and to add to her dower the sum of five thousand ducats, which I would give him when the deed was signed.

"I will mortgage them," said he, "on a house which is worth double."

Then turning to Leonilda, who was shedding happy tears, he said,—

"I am going to send for your mother, who will be delighted to sign the settlement, and to make the acquaintance of your future husband."

The mother lived at the Marquis Galiani's, a day's journey from Naples. The duke said he would send a carriage for her the next day, and that we could all sup together the day after.

"The law business will be all done by then, and we shall be able to go to the little church at Portici, and the priest will marry you. Then we will take your mother to St. Agatha and dine with her, and you can go your way with her maternal blessing."

This conclusion gave me an involuntary shudder, and Leonilda fell fainting in the duke's arms. He called her dear child, cared for her tenderly, and brought her to herself.

We all had to wipe our eyes, as we were all equally affected.

I considered myself as a married man and under obligation to alter my way of living, and I stopped playing. I had won more than fifteen thousand ducats, and this sum added to what I had before and Leonilda's dowry should have sufficed for an honest livelihood.

Next day, as I was at supper with the duke and Leonilda, she said,—

"What will my mother say to-morrow evening, when she sees you?"

"She will say that you are silly to marry a stranger whom you have only known for a week. Have you told her my name, my nation, my condition, and my age?"

"I wrote to her as follows:

"'Dear mamma, come directly and sign my marriage contract with a gentleman introduced to me by the duke, with whom I shall be leaving for Rome on Monday next.'"

"My letter ran thus," said the duke,

"'Come without delay, and sign your daughter's marriage contract, and give her your blessing. She has wisely chosen a husband old enough to be her father; he is a friend of mine.'"

"That's not true," cried Leonilda, rushing to my arms, "she will think you are really old, and I am sorry."

"Is your mother an elderly woman?"

"She's a charming woman," said the duke, "full of wit, and not thirty-eight yet."

"What has she got to do with Galiani?"

"She is an intimate friend of the marchioness's, and she lives with the family but pays for her board."

Next morning, having some business with my banker to attend to, I told the duke that I should not be able to see Leonilda till supper-time. I went there at eight o'clock and I found the three sitting in front of the fire.

"Here he is!" cried the duke.

As soon as the mother saw me she screamed and fell nearly fainting on a chair. I looked at her fixedly for a minute, and exclaimed,—

"Donna Lucrezia! I am fortunate indeed!"

"Let us take breath, my dear friend. Come and sit by me. So you are going to marry my daughter, are you?"

I took a chair and guessed it all. My hair stood on end, and I relapsed into a gloomy silence.

The stupefied astonishment of Leonilda and the duke cannot be described. They could see that Donna Lucrezia and I knew each other, but they could not get any farther. As for myself, as I pondered gloomily and compared Leonilda's age with the period at which I had been intimate with Lucrezia Castelli, I could see that it was quite possible that she might be my daughter; but I told myself that the mother could not be certain of the fact, as at the time she lived with her husband, who was very fond of her and not fifty years of age. I could bear the suspense no longer, so, taking a light and begging Leonilda and the duke to excuse me, I asked Lucrezia to come into the next room with me.

As soon as she was seated, she drew me to her and said,—

"Must I grieve my dear one when I have loved so well? Leonilda is your daughter, I am certain of it. I always looked upon her as your daughter, and my husband knew it, but far from being angry, he used to adore her. I will shew you the register of her birth, and

58

you can calculate for yourself. My husband was at Rome, and did not see me once, and my daughter did not come before her time. You must remember a letter which my mother should have given you, in which I told you I was with child. That was in January, 1744, and in six months my daughter will be seventeen. My late husband gave her the names of Leonilda Giacomina at the baptismal font, and when he played with her he always called her by the latter name. This idea of your marrying her horrifies me, but I cannot oppose it, as I am ashamed to tell the reason. What do you think? Have you still the courage to marry her? You seem to hesitate. Have you taken any earnest of the marriage-bed?"

"No, dear Lucrezia, your daughter is as pure as a lily."

"I breathe again."

"Ah, yes! but my heart is torn asunder."

"I am grieved to see you thus."

"She has no likeness to me."

"That proves nothing; she has taken after me. You are weeping, dearest, you will break my heart."

"Who would not weep in my place? I will send the duke to you; he must know all."

I left Lucrezia, and I begged the duke to go and speak to her. The affectionate Leonilda came and sat on my knee, and asked me what the dreadful mystery was. I was too much affected to be able to answer her; she kissed me, and we began to weep. We remained thus sad and silent till the return of the duke and Donna Lucrezia, who was the only one to keep her head cool.

"Dear Leonilda," said she, "you must be let into the secret of this disagreeable mystery, and your mother is the proper person to enlighten you. Do you remember what name my late husband used to call you when he petted you?"

"He used to call me his charming Giacomina."

"That is M. Casanova's name; it is the name of your father. Go and kiss him; his blood flows in your veins; and if he has been your lover, repent of the crime which was happily quite involuntary."

The scene was a pathetic one, and we were all deeply moved. Leonilda clung to her mother's knees, and in a voice that struggled with sobs exclaimed,—

"I have only felt what an affectionate daughter might feel for a father."

At this point silence fell on us, a silence that was only broken by the sobs of the two women, who held each other tightly embraced; while the duke and I sat as motionless as two posts, our heads bent and our hands crossed, without as much as looking at each other.

Supper was served, and we sat at table for three hours, talking sadly over this dramatic recognition, which had brought more grief than joy; and we departed at midnight full of melancholy, and hoping that we should be calmer on the morrow, and able to take the only step that now remained to us.

As we were going away the duke made several observations on what moral philosophers call prejudices. There is no philosopher who would maintain or even advance the thesis that the union of a father and daughter is horrible naturally, for it is entirely a social prejudice; but it is so widespread, and education has graven it so deeply in our hearts, that only a man whose heart is utterly depraved could despise it. It is the result of a respect for the laws, it keeps the social scheme together; in fact, it is no longer a prejudice, it is a principle.

I went to bed, but as usual, after the violent emotion I had undergone, I could not sleep. The rapid transition from carnal to paternal love cast my physical and mental faculties into such a state of excitement that I could scarcely withstand the fierce struggle that was taking place in my heart.

Towards morning I fell asleep for a short time, and woke up feeling as exhausted as two lovers who have been spending a long and voluptuous winter's night.

When I got up I told the duke that I intended to set out from Naples the next day; and he observed that as everybody knew I was on the eve of my departure, this haste would make people talk.

"Come and have some broth with me," said he; "and from henceforth look upon this marriage project as one of the many pranks in which you have engaged. We will spend the three or four days pleasantly together, and perhaps when we have thought over all this for some time we shall end by thinking it matter for mirth and not sadness. Believe me the mother's as good as the daughter; recollection is often better than hope; console yourself with Lucrezia. I don't think you can see any difference between her present appearance and that of eighteen years ago, for I don't see how she can ever have been handsomer than she is now."

This remonstrance brought me to my senses. I felt that the best thing I could do would be to forget the illusion which had amused me for four or five days, and as my self-esteem was not wounded it ought not to be a difficult task; but yet I was in love and unable to satisfy my love.

Love is not like merchandise, where one can substitute one thing for another when one cannot have what one wants. Love is a sentiment, only the object who has kindled the flame can soothe the heat thereof.

We went to call on my daughter, the duke in his usual mood, but I looking pale, depressed, weary, and like a boy going to receive the rod. I was extremely surprised when I came into the room to find the mother and daughter quite gay, but this helped on my cure. Leonilda threw her arms round my neck, calling me dear papa, and kissing me with all a daughter's freedom. Donna Lucrezia stretched out her hand, addressing me as her dear friend. I regarded her attentively, and I was forced to confess that the eighteen years that had passed away had done little ill to her charms. There was the same sparkling glance, that fresh complexion, those perfect shapes, those beautiful lips—in fine, all that had charmed my youthful eyes.

We mutely caressed each other. Leonilda gave and received the tenderest kisses without seeming to notice what desires she might cause to arise; no doubt she knew that as her father I should have strength to resist, and she was right. One gets used to everything, and I was ashamed to be sad any longer.

I told Donna Lucrezia of the curious welcome her sister had given me in Rome, and she went off into peals of laughter. We reminded each other of the night at Tivoli, and these recollections softened our hearts. From these softened feelings to love is but a short way; but neither place nor time were convenient, so we pretended not to be thinking of it.

After a few moments of silence I told her that if she cared to come to Rome with me to pay a visit to her sister Angelique, I would take her back to Naples at the beginning of Lent. She promised to let me know whether she could come on the following day.

I sat between her and Leonilda at dinner; and as I could no longer think of the daughter, it was natural that my old flame for Lucrezia should rekindle; and whether from the effect of her gaiety and beauty, or from my need of someone to love, or from the excellence of the wine, I found myself in love with her by the dessert, and asked her to take the place which her daughter was to have filled.

"I will marry you," said I, "and we will all of us go to Rome on Monday, for since Leonilda is my daughter I do not like to leave her at Naples."

At this the three guests looked at each other and said nothing. I did not repeat my proposal, but led the conversation to some other topic.

After dinner I felt sleepy and lay down on a bed, and did not wake till eight o'clock, when to my surprise I found that my only companion was Lucrezia, who was writing. She heard me stir, and came up to me and said affectionately,—

"My dear friend, you have slept for five hours; and as I did not like to leave you alone I would not go with the duke and our daughter to the opera."

The memory of former loves awakens when one is near the once beloved object, and desires rapidly become irresistible if the beauty still remain. The lovers feel as if they were once more in possession of a blessing which belongs to them, and of which they have been long deprived by unfortunate incidents. These were our feelings, and without delay, without idle discussion, and above all, without false modesty, we abandoned ourselves to love, the only true source of nature.

In the first interval, I was the first to break the silence; and if a man is anything of a wit, is he the less so at that delicious moment of repose which follows on an amorous victory?

"Once again, then," said I, "I am in this charming land which I entered for the first time to the noise of the drum and the rattle of musket shots."

This remark made her laugh, and recalled past events to her memory. We recollected with delight all the pleasures we had enjoyed at Testaccio, Frascati, and Tivoli. We reminded each other of these events, only to make each other laugh; but with two lovers, what is laughter but a pretext for renewing the sweet sacrifice of the goddess of Cythera?

At the end of the second act, full of the enthusiasm of the fortunate lover, I said,—

"Let us be united for life; we are of the same age, we love each other, our means are sufficient for us, we may hope to live a happy life, and to die at the same moment."

"'Tis the darling wish of my heart," Lucrezia replied, "but let us stay at Naples and leave Leonilda to the duke. We will see company, find her a worthy husband, and our happiness will be complete."

"I cannot live at Naples, dearest, and you know that your daughter intended to leave with me."

"My daughter! Say our daughter. I see that you are still in love with her, and do not wish to be considered her father."

"Alas, yes! But I am sure that if I live with you my passion for her will be stilled, but otherwise I cannot answer for myself. I shall fly, but flight will not bring me happiness. Leonilda charms me still more by her intelligence than by her beauty. I was sure that she loved me so well that I did not attempt to seduce her, lest thereby I should weaken my hold on her affections; and as I wanted to make her happy I wished to deserve her esteem. I longed to possess her, but in a lawful manner, so that our rights should have been equal. We have created an angel, Lucrezia, and I cannot imagine how the duke . . ."

"The duke is completely impotent. Do you see now how I was able to trust my daughter to his care?"

"Impotent? I always thought so myself, but he has a son."

"His wife might possibly be able to explain that mystery to you, but you may take it for granted that the poor duke will die a virgin in spite of himself; and he knows that as well as anybody."

"Do not let us say any more about it, but allow me to treat you as at
Tivoli."

"Not just now, as I hear carriage wheels."

A moment after the door opened, and Leonilda laughed heartily to see her mother in my arms, and threw herself upon us, covering us with kisses. The duke came in a little later, and we supped together very merrily. He thought me the happiest of men when I told him I was going to pass the night honourably with my wife and daughter; and he was right, for I was so at that moment.

As soon as the worthy man left us we went to bed, but here I must draw a veil over the most voluptuous night I have ever spent. If I told all I should wound chaste ears, and, besides, all the colours of the painter and all the phrases of the poet could not do justice to the delirium of pleasure, the ecstasy, and the license which passed during that night, while two wax lights burnt dimly on the table like candles before the shrine of a saint.

We did not leave the stage, which I watered with my blood, till long after the sun had risen. We were scarcely dressed when the duke arrived.

Leonilda gave him a vivid description of our nocturnal labours, but in his unhappy state of impotence he must have been thankful for his absence.

I was determined to start the next day so as to be at Rome for the last week of the carnival and I begged the duke to let me give Leonilda the five thousand ducats which would have been her dower if she had become my bride.

"As she is your daughter," said he, "she can and ought to take this present from her father, if only as a dowry for her future husband."

"Will you accept it, then, my dear Leonilda?"

"Yes, papa dear," she said, embracing me, "on the condition that you will promise to come and see me again as soon as you hear of my marriage."

I promised to do so, and I kept my word.

"As you are going to-morrow," said the duke, "I shall ask all the nobility of Naples to meet you at supper. In the meanwhile I leave you with your daughter; we shall see each other again at suppertime."

He went out and I dined with my wife and daughter in the best of spirits. I spent almost the whole afternoon with Leonilda, keeping within the bounds of decency, less, perhaps, out of respect to morality, than because of my labours of the night before. We did not kiss each other till the moment of parting, and I could see that both mother and daughter were grieved to lose me.

After a careful toilette I went to supper, and found an assembly of a hundred of the very best people in Naples. The duchess was very agreeable, and when I kissed her hand to take leave, she said,

"I hope, Don Giacomo, that you have had no unpleasantness during your short stay at Naples, and that you will sometimes think of your visit with pleasure."

I answered that I could only recall my visit with delight after the kindness with which she had deigned to treat me that evening; and, in fact, my recollections of Naples were always of the happiest description.

After I had treated the duke's attendants with generosity, the poor nobleman, whom fortune had favoured, and whom nature had deprived of the sweetest of all enjoyments, came with me to the door of my carriage and I went on my way.

CHAPTER X

My Carriage Broken—Mariuccia's Wedding-Flight of Lord Lismore—My Return to Florence, and My Departure with the Corticelli

My Spaniard was going on before us on horseback, and I was sleeping profoundly beside Don Ciccio Alfani in my comfortable carriage, drawn by four horses, when a violent shock aroused me. The carriage had been overturned on the highway, at midnight, beyond Francolisa and four miles from St. Agatha.

Alfani was beneath me and uttered piercing shrieks, for he thought he had broken his left arm. Le Duc rode back and told me that the postillions had taken flight, possibly to give notice of our mishap to highwaymen, who are very common in the States of the Church and Naples.

I got out of the carriage easily enough, but poor old Alfani, who was unwieldly with fat, badly hurt, and half dead with fright, could not extricate himself without assistance. It took us a quarter of an hour to get him free. The poor wretch amused me by the blasphemies which he mingled with prayers to his patron saint, St. Francis of Assisi.

I was not without experience of such accidents and was not at all hurt, for one's safety depends a good deal on the position one is in. Don Ciccio had probably hurt his arm by stretching it out just as the accident took place.

I took my sword, my musket, and my horse-pistols out of the carriage, and I made them and my pockets pistols ready so as to offer a stiff resistance to the brigands if they came; and I then told Le Duc to take some money and ride off and see if he could bring some peasants to our assistance.

Don Ciccio groaned over the accident, but I, resolving to sell my money and my life dearly, made a rampart of the carriage and four horses, and stood sentry, with my arms ready.

I then felt prepared for all hazards, and was quite calm, but my unfortunate companion continued to pour forth his groans, and prayers, and blasphemies, for all that goes together at Naples as at Rome. I could do nothing but compassionate him; but in spite of myself I could not help laughing, which seemed to vex the poor abbe, who looked for all the world like a dying dolphin as he rested motionless against the bank. His distress may be imagined, when the nearest horse yielded to the call of nature, and voided over the unfortunate man the contents of its bladder. There was nothing to be done, and I could not help roaring with laughter.

Nevertheless, a strong northerly wind rendered our situation an extremely unpleasant one. At the slightest noise I cried, "Who goes there?" threatening to fire on anyone who dared approach. I spent two hours in this tragic-comic position, until at last Le Duc rode up and told me that a band of peasants, all armed and provided with lanterns, were approaching to our assistance.

In less than an hour, the carriage, the horses, and Alfani were seen to. I kept two of the country-folk to serve as postillions, and I sent the others away well paid for the interruption of their sleep. I reached St. Agatha at day-break, and I made the devil's own noise at the door of the postmaster, calling for an attorney to take down my statement, and threatening to have the postillions who had overturned and deserted me, hanged.

A wheelwright inspected my coach and pronounced the axle-tree broken, and told me I should have to remain for a day at least.

Don Ciccio, who stood in need of a surgeon's aid, called on the Marquis Galliani without telling me anything about it. However, the marquis hastened to beg me to stay at his home till I could continue my journey. I accepted the invitation with great pleasure, and with this my ill humour, which was really only the result of my desire to make a great fuss like a great man, evaporated.

The marquis ordered my carriage to be taken to his coach-house, took me by the arm, and led me to his house. He was as learned as he was polite, and a perfect Neapolitan—i.e., devoid of all ceremony. He had not the brilliant wit of his brother, whom I had known at Paris as secretary of embassy under the Count Cantillana Montdragon, but he possessed a well-ordered judgment, founded on study and the perusal of ancient and modern classics. Above all, he was a great mathematician, and was then preparing an annotated edition of Vitruvius, which was afterwards published.

The marquis introduced me to his wife, whom I knew as the intimate friend of my dear Lucrezia. There was something saint-like in her expression, and to see her surrounded by her little children was like looking at a picture of the Holy Family.

Don Ciccio was put to bed directly, and a surgeon sent for, who consoled him by saying that it was only a simple luxation, and that he would be well again in a few days.

At noon a carriage stopped at the door, and Lucrezia got down. She embraced the marchioness, and said to me in the most natural manner, as we shook hands,—

"What happy chance brings you hear, dear Don Giacomo?"

She told her friend that I was a friend of her late husband's, and that she had recently seen me again with great pleasure at the Duke de Matalone's.

After dinner, on finding myself alone with this charming woman, I asked her if it were not possible for us to pass a happy night together, but she shewed me that it was out of the question, and I had to yield. I renewed my offer to marry her.

"Buy a property," said she, "in the kingdom of Naples, and I will spend the remainder of my days with you, without asking a priest to give us his blessing, unless we happen to have children."

I could not deny that Lucrezia spoke very sensibly, and I could easily have bought land in Naples, and lived comfortably on it, but the idea of binding myself down to one place was so contrary to my feelings that I had the good sense to prefer my vagabond life to all the advantages which our union would have given me, and I do not think that Lucrezia altogether disapproved of my resolution.

After supper I took leave of everybody, and I set out at day-break in order to get to Rome by the next day. I had only fifteen stages to do, and the road was excellent.

As we were getting into Carillano, I saw one of the two-wheeled carriages, locally called mantice, two horses were being put into it, while my carriage required four. I got out, and on hearing myself called I turned round. I was not a little surprised to find that the occupants of the mantice were a young and pretty girl and Signora Diana, the Prince de Sassaro's mistress, who owed me three hundred ounces. She told me that she was going to Rome, and that she would be glad if we could make the journey together.

"I suppose you don't mind stopping for the night at Piperno?"

"No," said I, "I am afraid that can't be managed; I don't intend to break my journey."

"But you would get to Rome by to-morrow."

"I know that, but I sleep better in my carriage than in the bad beds they give you in the inns."

"I dare not travel by night."

"Well, well, madam, I have no doubt we shall see each other at Rome."

"You are a cruel man. You see I have only a stupid servant, and a maid who is as timid as I am, besides it is cold and my carriage is open. I will keep you company in yours."

"I really can't take you in, as all the available space is taken up by my old secretary, who broke his arm yesterday."

"Shall we dine together at Terracino? We could have a little talk."

"Certainly."

We made good cheer at this small town, which is the frontier of the States of the Church. We should not reach Piperno till far on in the night, and the lady renewed and redoubled her efforts to keep me till daybreak; but though young and pretty she did not take my fancy; she was too fair and too fat. But her maid, who was a pretty brunette, with a delicious rounded form and a sparkling eye, excited all my feelings of desire. A vague hope of possessing the maid won me over, and I ended by promising the signora to sup with her, and not to continue my journey without giving notice to the landlord.

When we got to Piperno, I succeeded in telling the pretty maid that if she would let me have her quietly I would not go any further. She promised to wait for me, and allowed me to take such liberties as are usually the signs of perfect complaisance.

We had our supper, and I wished the ladies good night and escorted them to their room, where I took note of the relative positions of their beds so that there should be no mistake. I left them and came back in a quarter of an hour. Finding the door open I felt sure of success, and I got into bed; but as I found out, it was the signora and not the maid who received me. Evidently the little hussy had told her mistress the story, and the mistress had thought fit to take the maid's place. There was no possibility of my being mistaken, for though I could not see I could feel.

For a moment I was undecided, should I remain in bed and make the best of what I had got, or go on my way to Rome immediately? The latter counsel prevailed. I called Le Duc, gave my orders, and started, enjoying the thought of the confusion of the two women, who must have been in a great rage at the failure of their plans. I saw Signora Diana three or four times at Rome, and we bowed without speaking; if I had thought it likely that she would pay me the four hundred louis she owed me I might have taken the trouble to call on her, but I know that your stage queens are the worst debtors in the world.

My brother, the Chevalier Mengs, and the Abbe Winckelmann were all in good health and spirits. Costa was delighted to see me again. I sent him off directly to His Holiness's 'scopatore maggiore' to warn him that I was coming to take polenta with him, and all he need do was to get a good supper for twelve. I was sure of finding Mariuccia there, for I knew that Momolo had noticed her presence pleased me.

The carnival began the day after my arrival, and I hired a superb landau for the whole week. The Roman landaus seat four people and have a hood which may be lowered at pleasure. In these landaus one drives along the Corso with or without masks from nine to twelve o'clock during the carnival time.

From time immemorial the Corso at Rome has presented a strange and diverting spectacle during the carnival. The horses start from the Piazza del Popolo, and gallop along to the Column of Trajan, between two lines of carriages drawn up beside two narrow pavements which are crowded with maskers and people of all classes. All the windows are decorated. As soon as the horses have passed the carriages begin to move, and the maskers on foot and horseback occupy the middle of the street. The air is full of real and false sweetmeats, pamphlets, pasquinades, and puns. Throughout the mob, composed of the best and worst classes of Rome, liberty reigns supreme, and when twelve o'clock is announced by the third report of the cannon of St. Angelo the Corso begins to clear, and in five minutes you would look in vain for a carriage or a masker. The crowd disperses amongst the neighbouring streets, and fills the opera houses, the theatres, the rope-dancers' exhibitions, and even the puppet-shows. The restaurants and taverns are not left desolate; everywhere you will find crowds of people, for during the carnival the Romans only think of eating, drinking, and enjoying themselves.

I banked my money with M. Belloni and got a letter of credit on Turin, where I expected to find the Abbe Gama and to receive a commission to represent the Portuguese Court at the Congress of Augsburg, to which all Europe was looking forward, and then I went to inspect my little room, where I hoped to meet Mariuccia the next day. I found everything in good order.

In the evening Momolo and his family received me with joyful exclamations. The eldest daughter said with a smile that she was sure she would please me by sending for Mariuccia.

"You are right," said I, "I shall be delighted to see the fair Mariuccia."

A few minutes after she entered with her puritanical mother, who told me I must not be surprised to see her daughter better dressed, as she was going to be married in a few days. I congratulated her, and Momolo's daughters asked who was the happy man. Mariuccia blushed and said modestly, to one of them,—

"It is somebody whom you know, So and so, he saw me here, and we are going to open a hair-dresser's shop."

"The marriage was arranged by good Father St. Barnabe," added the   mother.
"He has in his keeping my daughter's dower of four hundred Roman crowns."

"He's a good lad," said Momolo. "I have a high opinion of him; he would have married one of my daughters if I could have given him such a dowry."

At these words the girl in question blushed and lowered her eyes.

"Never mind, my dear," said I, "your turn will come in time."

She took my words as seriously meant, and her face lit up with joy. She thought I had guessed her love for Costa, and her idea was confirmed when I told him to get my landau the next day and take out all Momolo's daughters, well masked, as it would not do for them to be recognized in a carriage I meant to make use of myself. I also bade him hire some handsome costumes from a Jew, and paid the hire-money myself. This put them all in a good humour.

"How about Signora Maria?" said the jealous sister.

"As Signora Maria is going to be married," I replied, "she must not be present at any festivity without her future husband."

The mother applauded this decision of mine, and sly Mariuccia pretended to feel mortified. I turned to Momolo and begged him to ask Mariuccia's future husband to meet me at supper, by which I pleased her mother greatly.

I felt very tired, and having nothing to keep me after seeing Mariuccia, I begged the company to excuse me, and after wishing them a good appetite I left them.

I walked out next morning at an early hour. I had no need of going into the church, which I reached at seven o'clock, for Mariuccia saw me at some distance off and followed me, and we were soon alone together in the little room, which love and voluptuous pleasure had transmuted into a sumptuous place. We would gladly have talked to each other, but as we had only an hour before us, we set to without even taking off our clothes. After the last kiss which ended the third assault, she told me that she was to be married on the eve of Shrove Tuesday, and that all had been arranged by her confessor. She also thanked me for having asked Momolo to invite her intended.

"When shall we see each other again, my angel?"

"On Sunday, the eve of my wedding, we shall be able to spend four hours together."

"Delightful! I promise you that when you leave me you will be in such a state that the caresses of your husband won't hurt you."

She smiled and departed, and I threw myself on the bed where I rested for a good hour.

As I was going home I met a carriage and four going at a great speed. A footman rode in front of the carriage, and within it I saw a young nobleman. My attention was arrested by the blue ribbon on his breast. I gazed at him, and he called out my name and had the carriage stopped. I was extremely surprised when I found it was Lord O'Callaghan, whom I had known at Paris at his mother's, the Countess of Lismore, who was separated from her husband, and was the kept mistress of M. de St. Aubin, the unworthy successor of the good and virtuous Fenelon in the archbishopric of Cambrai. However, the archbishop owed his promotion to the fact that he was a bastard of the Duc d'Orleans, the French Regent.

Lord O'Callaghan was a fine-looking young man, with wit and talent, but the slave of his unbridled passions and of every species of vice. I knew that if he were lord in name he was not so in fortune, and I was astonished to see him driving such a handsome carriage, and still more so at his blue ribbon. In a few words he told me that he was going to dine with the Pretender, but that he would sup at home. He invited me to come to supper, and I accepted.

After dinner I took a short walk, and then went to enliven myself at the theatre, where I saw Momolo's girls strutting about with Costa; afterwards I went to Lord O'Callaghan, and was pleasantly surprised to meet the poet Poinsinet. He was young, short, ugly, full of poetic fire, a wit, and dramatist. Five or six years later the poor fellow fell into the Guadalquivir and was drowned. He had gone to Madrid in the hope of making his fortune. As I had known him at Paris I addressed him as an old acquaintance.

"What are you doing at Rome? Where's my Lord O'Callaghan?"

"He's in the next room, but as his father is dead his title is now Earl of Lismore. You know he was an adherent of the Pretender's. I left Paris with him, well enough pleased at being able to come to Rome without its costing me anything."

"Then the earl is a rich man now?"

"Not exactly; but he will be, as he is his father's heir, and the old earl left an immense fortune. It is true that it is all confiscated, but that is nothing, as his claims are irresistible."

"In short, he is rich in claims and rich in the future; but how did he get himself made a knight of one of the French king's orders?"

"You're joking. That is the blue ribbon of the Order of St. Michael, of which the late Elector of Cologne was grand master. As you know, my lord plays exquisitely on the violin, and when he was at Bonn he played the Elector a concerto by Tartini. The prince could not find words in which to express the pleasure of my lord's performance, and gave him the ribbon you have seen."

"A fine present, doubtless."

"You don't know what pleasure it gave my lord, for when we go back to Paris everybody will take it for the Order of the Holy Ghost."

We passed into a large room, where we found the earl with the party he had asked to supper. As soon as he saw me he embraced me, called me his dear friend, and named his guests. There were seven or eight girls, all of them pretty, three or four castrati who played women's parts in the Roman theatre, and five or six abbes, the husband of every wife and the wives of every husband, who boasted of their wickedness, and challenged the girls to be more shameless than they. The girls were not common courtezans, but past mistresses of music, painting, and vice considered as a fine art. The kind of society may be imagined when I say that I found myself a perfect novice amongst them.

"Where are you going, prince?" said the earl to a respectable-looking man who was making for the door.

"I don't feel well, my lord. I think I must go out."

"What prince is that?" said I.

"The Prince de Chimai. He is a sub-deacon, and is endeavouring to gain permission to marry, lest his family should become extinct."

"I admire his prudence or his delicacy, but I am afraid I should not imitate him."

There were twenty-four of us at table, and it is no exaggeration to say that we emptied a hundred bottles of the choicest wines. Everybody was drunk, with the exception of myself and the poet Poinsinet, who had taken nothing but water. The company rose from table, and then began a foul orgy which I should never have conceived possible, and which no pen could describe, though possibly a seasoned profligate might get some idea of it.

A castrato and a girl of almost equal height proposed to strip in an adjoining room, and to lie on their backs, in the same bed with their faces covered. They challenged us all to guess which was which.

We all went in and nobody could pronounce from sight which was male and which was female, so I bet the earl fifty crowns that I would point out the woman.

He accepted the wager, and I guessed correctly, but payment was out of the question.

This first act of the orgy ended with the prostitution of the two individuals, who defied everybody to accomplish the great act. All, with the exception of Poinsinet and myself, made the attempt, but their efforts were in vain.

The second act displayed four or five couples reversed, and here the abbes shone, both in the active and passive parts of this lascivious spectacle. I was the only person respected.

All at once, the earl, who had hitherto remained perfectly motionless, attacked the wretched Poinsinet, who in vain attempted to defend himself. He had to strip like my lord, who was as naked as the others. We stood round in a circle. Suddenly the earl, taking his watch, promised it to the first who succeeded in giving them a sure mark of sensibility. The desire of gaining the prize excited the impure crowd immensely, and the castrati, the girls, and the abbes all did their utmost, each one striving to be the first. They had to draw lots. This part interested me most, for throughout this almost incredible scene of debauchery I did not experience the slightest sensation, although under other circumstances any of the girls would have claimed my homage, but all I did was to laugh, especially to see the poor poet in terror of experiencing the lust of the flesh, for the profligate nobleman swore that if he made him lose he would deliver him up to the brutal lust of all the abbes. He escaped, probably through fear of the consequences.

The orgy came to an end when nobody had any further hopes of getting the watch. The secret of the Lesbians was only employed, however, by the abbes and the castrata. The girls, wishing to be able to despise those who made use of it, refrained from doing so. I suspect they were actuated by pride rather than shame, as they might possibly have employed it without success.

This vile debauch disgusted me, and yet gave me a better knowledge of myself. I could not help confessing that my life had been endangered, for the only arm I had was my sword, but I should certainly have used it if the earl had tried to treat me like the others, and as he had treated poor Poinsinet. I never understood how it was that he respected me, for he was quite drunk, and in a kind of Bacchic fury.

As I left, I promised to come and see him as often as he pleased, but I promised myself never to set foot in his house again.

Next day, he came to see me in the afternoon, and asked me to walk with him to the Villa Medici.

I complimented him on the immense wealth he had inherited to enable him to live so splendidly, but he laughed and told me that he did not possess fifty piastres, that his father had left nothing but debts, and that he himself already owed three or four thousand crowns.

"I wonder people give you credit, then."

"They give me credit because everybody knows that I have drawn a bill of exchange on Paris to the tune of two hundred thousand francs. But in four or five days the bill will be returned protested, and I am only waiting for that to happen to make my escape."

"If you are certain of its being protested, I advise you to make your escape to-day; for as it is so large a sum it may be taken up before it is due."

"No, I won't do that; I have one hope left. I have written to tell my mother that I shall be undone if she does not furnish the banker, on whom I have drawn the bill, with sufficient funds and if she does that, the bill will be accepted. You know my mother is very fond of me."

"Yes, but I also know that she is far from rich."

"True, but M. de St. Aubin is rich enough, and between you and me I think he is my father. Meanwhile, my creditors are almost as quiet as I am. All those girls you saw yesterday would give me all they have if I asked them, as they are all expecting me to make them a handsome present in the course of the week, but I won't abuse their trust in me. But I am afraid I shall be obliged to cheat the Jew, who wants me to give him three thousand sequins for this ring, as I know it is only worth one thousand."

"He will send the police after you."

"I defy him to do whatever he likes."

The ring was set with a straw-coloured diamond of nine or ten carats. He begged me to keep his secret as we parted. I did not feel any sentiments of pity for this extravagant madman, as I only saw in him a man unfortunate by his own fault, whose fate would probably make him end his days in a prison unless he had the courage to blow his brains out.

I went to Momolo's in the evening, and found the intended husband of my fair Mariuccia there, but not the lady herself. I heard she had sent word to the 'scopatore santissimo' that, as her father had come from Palestrina to be present at her wedding, she could not come to supper. I admired her subtlety. A young girl has no need of being instructed in diplomacy, nature and her own heart are her teachers, and she never blunders. At supper I studied the young man, and found him eminently suitable for Mariuccia; he was handsome, modest, and intelligent, and whatever he said was spoken frankly and to the point.

He told me before Momolo's daughter, Tecla, that he would have married her if she had possessed means to enable him to open his shop, and that he had reason to thank God for having met Maria, whose confessor had been such a true spiritual father to her. I asked him where the wedding festivities were to take place, and he told me they were to be at his father's house, on the other side of the Tiber. As his father, who kept a garden, was poor, he had furnished him with ten crowns to defray the expenses.

I wanted to give him the ten crowns, but how was I to do it? It would have betrayed me.

"Is your father's garden a pretty one?" I asked.

"Not exactly pretty, but very well kept. As he owns the land, he has separated a plot which he wants to sell; it would bring in twenty crowns a year, and I should be as happy as a cardinal if I could buy it."

"How much will it cost?"

"It's a heavy price; two hundred crowns."

"Why, that's cheap! Listen to me. I have met your future bride at this house, and I have found her all worthy of happiness. She deserves an honest young fellow like you for a husband. Now what would you do supposing I were to make you a present of two hundred crowns to buy the garden?"

"I should put it to my wife's dowry."

"Then here are the two hundred crowns. I shall give them to Momolo, as I don't know you well enough, though I think you are perfectly to be trusted. The garden is yours, as part of your wife's dowry."

Momolo took the money, and promised to buy the garden the following day, and the young man shedding tears of joy and gratitude fell on his knees and kissed my hand. All the girls wept, as I myself did, for there's a contagion in such happy tears. Nevertheless, they did not all proceed from the same source; some were virtuous and some vicious, and the young man's were the only ones whose source was pure and unalloyed. I lifted him from the ground, kissed him, and wished him a happy marriage. He made bold to ask me to his wedding, but I refused, thanking him kindly. I told him that if he wanted to please me, he must come and sup at Momolo's on the eve of his wedding, and I begged the good scopatore to ask Mariuccia, her father and mother as well. I was sure of seeing her for the last time on the Sunday morning.

At seven o'clock on the Sunday morning we were in each other's arms, with four hours before us. After the first burst of mutual ardour she told me that all arrangements had been made in her house the evening before, in the presence of her confessor and of Momolo; and that on the receipt for the two hundred crowns being handed in the notary had put the garden into the settlement, and that the good father had made her a present of twenty piastres towards defraying the notary's fees and the wedding expenses.

"Everything is for the best, and I am sure I shall be happy. My intended adores you, but you did wisely not to accept his invitation, for you would have found everything so poor, and besides tongues might have been set wagging to my disadvantage."

"You are quite right, dearest, but what do you intend to do if your husband finds that the door has been opened by someone else, for possibly he expects you to be a maid."

"I expect he will know no more about it than I did the first time you knew me; besides, I do not feel that you have defiled me, and my clean conscience will not allow me to think of the matter; and I am sure that he will not think of it any more than I."

"Yes, but if he does?"

"It would not be delicate on his part, but what should prevent me from replying that I don't know what he means?"

"You are right; that's the best way. But have you told your confessor of our mutual enjoyment?"

"No, for as I did not give myself up to you with any criminal intention,
I do not think I have offended God."

"You are an angel, and I admire the clearness of your reasoning. But listen to me; it's possible that you are already with child, or that you may become so this morning; promise to name the child after me."

"I will do so."

The four hours sped rapidly away. After the sixth assault we were wearied though not satiated. We parted with tears, and swore to love each other as brother and sister ever after.

I went home, bathed, slept an hour, rose, dressed, and dined pleasantly with the family. In the evening I took the Mengs family for a drive in my landau, and we then went to the theatre, where the castrato who played the prima donna was a great attraction. He was the favourite pathic of Cardinal Borghese, and supped every evening with his eminence.

This castrato had a fine voice, but his chief attraction was his beauty. I had seen him in man's clothes in the street, but though a fine-looking fellow, he had not made any impression on me, for one could see at once that he was only half a man, but on the stage in woman's dress the illusion was complete; he was ravishing.

He was enclosed in a carefully-made corset and looked like a nymph; and incredible though it may seem, his breast was as beautiful as any woman's; it was the monster's chiefest charm. However well one knew the fellow's neutral sex, as soon as one looked at his breast one felt all aglow and quite madly amorous of him. To feel nothing one would have to be as cold and impassive as a German. As he walked the boards, waiting for the refrain of the air he was singing, there was something grandly voluptuous about him; and as he glanced towards the boxes, his black eyes, at once tender and modest, ravished the heart. He evidently wished to fan the flame of those who loved him as a man, and probably would not have cared for him if he had been a woman.

Rome the holy, which thus strives to make all men pederasts, denies the fact, and will not believe in the effects of the glamour of her own devising.

I made these reflections aloud, and an ecclesiastic, wishing to blind me to the truth, spoke as follows:—

"You are quite right. Why should this castrato be allowed to shew his breast, of which the fairest Roman lady might be proud, and yet wish everyone to consider him as a man and not a woman? If the stage is forbidden to the fair sex lest they excite desires, why do they seek out men-monsters made in the form of women, who excite much more criminal desires? They keep on preaching that pederasty is comparatively unknown and entraps only a few, but many clever men endeavour to be entrapped, and end by thinking it so pleasant that they prefer these monsters to the most beautiful women."

"The Pope would be sure of heaven if he put a stop to this scandalous practice."

"I don't agree with you. One could not have a pretty actress to supper without causing a scandal, but such an invitation to a castrato makes nobody talk. It is of course known perfectly well that after supper both heads rest on one pillow, but what everybody knows is ignored by all. One may sleep with a man out of mere friendship, it is not so with a woman."

"True, monsignor, appearances are saved, and a sin concealed is half pardoned, as they say in Paris."

"At Rome we say it is pardoned altogether. 'Peccato nascosto non offende'."

His jesuitical arguments interested me, for I knew that he was an avowed partisan of the forbidden fruit.

In one of the boxes I saw the Marchioness Passarini (whom I had known at Dresden) with Don Antonio Borghese, and I went to pay my addresses to them. The prince, whom I had known at Paris ten years before, recognized me, and asked me to dine with him on the following day. I went, but my lord was not at home. A page told me that my place was laid at table, and that I could dine just as if the prince was there, on which I turned my back on him and went away. On Ash Wednesday he sent his man to ask me to sup with him and the marchioness, who was his mistress, and I sent word that I would not fail to come; but he waited for me in vain. Pride is the daughter of folly, and always keeps its mother's nature.

After the opera I went to Momolo's, where I found Mariuccia, her father, her mother, and her future husband. They were anxiously expecting me. It is not difficult to make people happy when one selects for one's bounty persons who really deserve happiness. I was amidst poor but honest people, and I can truly say that I had a delightful supper. It may be that some of my enjoyment proceeded from a feeling of vanity, for I knew that I was the author of the happiness depicted on the faces of the bride and bridegroom and of the father and mother of Mariuccia; but when vanity causes good deeds it is a virtue. Nevertheless, I owe it to myself to tell my readers that my pleasure was too pure to have in it any admixture of vice.

After supper I made a small bank at faro, making everybody play with counters, as nobody had a penny, and I was so fortunate as to make everyone win a few ducats.

After the game we danced in spite of the prohibition of the Pope, whom no Roman can believe to be infallible, for he forbids dancing and permits games of chance. His successor Ganganelli followed the opposite course, and was no better obeyed. To avoid suspicion I did not give the pair any present, but I gave up my landau to them that they might enjoy the carnival on the Corso, and I told Costa to get them a box at the Capranica Theatre. Momolo asked me to supper on Shrove Tuesday.

I wished to leave Rome on the second day of Lent, and I called on the Holy Father at a time when all Rome was on the Corso. His Holiness welcomed me most graciously, and said he was surprised that I had not gone to see the sights on the Corso like everybody else. I replied that as a lover of pleasure I had chosen the greatest pleasure of all for a Christian—namely, to kneel at the feet of the vicar of Christ on earth. He bowed with a kind of majestic humility, which shewed me how the compliment had pleased him. He kept me for more than an hour, talking about Venice, Padua, and Paris, which latter city the worthy man would not have been sorry to have visited. I again commended myself to his apostolic intercession to enable me to return to my native country, and he replied,—

"Have recourse to God, dear son; His grace will be more efficacious than my prayers;" and then he blessed me and wished me a prosperous journey.

I saw that the Head of the Church had no great opinion of his own power.

On Shrove Tuesday I dressed myself richly in the costume of Polichinello, and rode along the Corso showering sweetmeats on all the pretty women I saw. Finally I emptied the basket on the daughters of the worthy 'scopatore', whom Costa was taking about in my landau with all the dignity of a pasha.

At night-time I took off my costume and went to Momolo's, where I expected to see dear Mariuccia for the last time. Supper passed off in almost a similar manner to the supper of last Sunday; but there was an interesting novelty for me—namely, the sight of my beloved mistress in her character of bride. Her husband seemed to be much more reserved with respect to me than at our first meeting. I was puzzled by his behaviour, and sat down by Mariuccia and proceeded to question her. She told me all the circumstances which had passed on the first night, and she spoke highly of her husband's good qualities. He was kind, amorous, good-tempered, and delicate. No doubt he must have noticed that the casket had been opened, but he had said nothing about it. As he had spoken about me, she had not been able to resist the pleasure of telling him that I was her sole benefactor, at which, so far from being offended, he seemed to trust in her more than ever.

"But has he not questioned you indirectly as to the connection between us?"

"Not at all. I told him that you went to my confessor after having spoken to me once only in the church, where I told you what a good chance I had of being married to him."

"Do you think he believed you?"

"I am not sure; however, even if it were otherwise, it is enough that he pretends to, for I am determined to win his esteem."

"You are right, and I think all the better of him for his suspicions, for it is better to marry a man with some sense in his head than to marry a fool."

I was so pleased with what she told me that when I took leave of the company I embraced the hairdresser, and drawing a handsome gold watch from my fob I begged him to accept it as a souvenir of me. He received it with the utmost gratitude. From my pocket I took a ring, worth at least six hundred francs, and put it on his wife's finger, wishing them a fair posterity and all manner of happiness, and I then went home to bed, telling Le Duc and Costa that we must begin to pack up next day.

I was just getting up when they brought me a note from Lord Lismore, begging me to come and speak to him at noon at the Villa Borghese.

I had some suspicion of what he might want, and kept the appointment. I felt in a mood to give him some good advice. Indeed, considering the friendship between his mother and myself, it was my duty to do so.

He came up to me and gave me a letter he had received the evening before from his mother. She told him that Paris de Monmartel had just informed her that he was in possession of a bill for two hundred thousand francs drawn by her son, and that he would honour it if she would furnish him with the funds. She had replied that she would let him know in two or three days if she could do so; but she warned her son that she had only asked for this delay to give him time to escape, as the bill would certainly be protested and returned, it being absolutely out of the question for her to get the money.

"You had better make yourself scarce as soon as you can," said I, returning him the letter.

"Buy this ring, and so furnish me with the means for my escape. You would not know that it was not my property if I had not told you so in confidence."

I made an appointment with him, and had the stone taken out and valued by one of the best jewellers in Rome.

"I know this stone," said he, "it is worth two thousand Roman crowns."

At four o'clock I took the earl five hundred crowns in gold and fifteen hundred crowns in paper, which he would have to take to a banker, who would give him a bill of exchange in Amsterdam.

"I will be off at nightfall," said he, "and travel by myself to Amsterdam, only taking such effects as are absolutely necessary, and my beloved blue ribbon."

"A pleasant journey to you," said I, and left him. In ten days I had the stone mounted at Bologna.

I got a letter of introduction from Cardinal Albani for Onorati, the nuncio at Florence, and another letter from M. Mengs to Sir Mann, whom he begged to receive me in his house. I was going to Florence for the sake of the Corticelli and my dear Therese, and I reckoned on the auditor's feigning to ignore my return, in spite of his unjust order, especially if I were residing at the English minister's.

On the second day of Lent the disappearance of Lord Lismore was the talk of the town. The English tailor was ruined, the Jew who owned the ring was in despair, and all the silly fellow's servants were turned out of the house in almost a state of nakedness, as the tailor had unceremoniously taken possession of everything in the way of clothes that he could lay his hands on.

Poor Poinsinet came to see me in a pitiable condition; he had only his shirt and overcoat. He had been despoiled of everything, and threatened with imprisonment. "I haven't a farthing," said the poor child of the muses, "I have only the shirt on my back. I know nobody here, and I think I shall go and throw myself into the Tiber."

He was destined, not to be drowned in the Tiber but in the Guadalquivir. I calmed him by offering to take him to Florence with me, but I warned him that I must leave him there, as someone was expecting me at Florence. He immediately took up his abode with me, and wrote verses incessantly till it was time to go.

My brother Jean made me a present of an onyx of great beauty. It was a cameo, representing Venus bathing, and a genuine antique, as the name of the artist, Sostrates, was cut on the stone. Two years later I sold it to Dr. Masti, at London, for three hundred pounds, and it is possibly still in the British Museum.

I went my way with Poinsinet who amused me, in spite of his sadness, with his droll fancies. In two days I got down at Dr. Vannini's, who tried to conceal his surprise at seeing me. I lost no time, but waited on Sir—— Mann immediately, and found him sitting at table. He gave me a very friendly reception, but he seemed alarmed when, in reply to his question, I told him that my dispute with the auditor had not been arranged. He told me plainly that he thought I had made a mistake in returning to Florence, and that he would be compromised by my staying with him. I pointed out that I was only passing through Florence.

"That's all very well," said he, "but you know you ought to call on the auditor."

I promised to do so, and returned to my lodging. I had scarcely shut the door, when an agent of police came and told me that the auditor had something to say to me, and would be glad to see me at an early hour next morning.

I was enraged at this order, and determined to start forthwith rather than obey. Full of this idea I called on Therese and found she was at Pisa. I then went to see the Corticelli, who threw her arms round my neck, and made use of the Bolognese grimaces appropriate to the occasion. To speak the truth, although the girl was pretty, her chief merit in my eyes was that she made me laugh.

I gave some money to her mother to get us a good supper, and I took the girl out on pretence of going for a walk. I went with her to my lodging, and left her with Poinsinet, and going to another room I summoned Costa and Vannini. I told Costa in Vannini's presence to go on with Le Duc and my luggage the following day, and to call for me at the "Pilgrim" at Bologna. I gave Vannini my instructions, and he left the room; and then I ordered Costa to leave Florence with Signora Laura and her son, and to tell them that I and the daughter were on in front. Le Duc received similar orders, and calling Poinsinet I gave him ten Louis, and begged him to look out for some other lodging that very evening. The worthy but unfortunate young man wept grateful tears, and told me that he would set out for Parma on foot next day, and that there M. Tillot would do some, thing for him.

I went back to the next room, and told the Corticelli to come with me. She did so under the impression that we were going back to her mother's, but without taking the trouble to undeceive her I had a carriage and pair got ready, and told the postillion to drive to Uccellatoio, the first post on the Bologna road.

"Where in the world are we going?" said she.

"Bologna."

"How about mamma?"

"She will come on to-morrow."

"Does she know about it?"

"No, but she will to-morrow when Costa comes to tell her, and to fetch her and your brother."

She liked the joke, and got into the carriage laughing, and we drove away.

CHAPTER XI

My Arrival at Bologna—I Am Expelled from Modena—I Visit Parma and Turin—The Pretty Jewess—The Dressmaker

The Corticelli had a good warm mantle, but the fool who carried her off had no cloak, even of the most meagre kind, to keep off the piercing cold, which was increased by a keen wind blowing right in our faces.

In spite of all I would not halt, for I was afraid I might be pursued and obliged to return, which would have greatly vexed me.

When I saw that the postillion was slackening his speed, I increased the amount of the present I was going to make him, and once more we rushed along at a headlong pace. I felt perishing with the cold; while the postillions seeing me so lightly clad, and so prodigal of my money to speed them on their way, imagined that I was a prince carrying off the heiress of some noble family. We heard them talking to this effect while they changed horses, and the Corticelli was so much amused that she did nothing but laugh for the rest of the way. In five hours we covered forty miles; we started from Florence at eight o'clock, and at one in the morning we stopped at a post in the Pope's territory, where I had nothing to fear. The stage goes under the name of "The Ass Unburdened."

The odd name of the inn made my mistress laugh afresh. Everybody was asleep, but the noise I made and the distribution of a few pauls procured me the privilege of a fire. I was dying of hunger, and they coolly told me there was nothing to eat. I laughed in the landlord's face, and told him to bring me his butter, his eggs, his macaroni, a ham, and some Parmesan cheese, for I knew that so much will be found in the inns all over Italy. The repast was soon ready, and I shewed the idiot host that he had materials for an excellent meal. We ate like four, and afterwards they made up an impromptu bed and we went to sleep, telling them to call me as soon as a carriage and four drew up.

Full of ham and macaroni, slightly warmed with the Chianti and Montepulciano, and tired with our journey, we stood more in need of slumber than of love, and so we gave ourselves up to sleep till morning. Then we gave a few moments to pleasure, but it was so slight an affair as not to be worth talking about.

At one o'clock we began to feel hungry again and got up, and the host provided us with an excellent dinner, after receiving instructions from me. I was astonished not to see the carriage draw up, but I waited patiently all day. Night came on and still no coach, and I began to feel anxious; but the Corticelli persisted in laughing at everything. Next morning I sent off an express messenger with instructions for Costa. In the event of any violence having taken place, I was resolved to return to Florence, of which city I could at any time make myself free by the expenditure of two hundred crowns.

The messenger started at noon, and returned at two o'clock with the news that my servants would shortly be with me. My coach was on its way, and behind it a smaller carriage with two horses, in which sat an old woman and a young man.

"That's the mother," said Corticelli; "now we shall have some fun. Let's get something for them to eat, and be ready to hear the history of this marvellous adventure which she will remember to her dying day."

Costa told me that the auditor had revenged my contempt of his orders by forbidding the post authorities to furnish any horses for my carriage. Hence the delay. But here we heard the allocution of the Signora Laura.

"I got an excellent supper ready," she began, "according to your orders; it cost me more than ten pauls, as I shall shew you, and I hope you will make it up to me as I'm but a poor woman. All was ready and I joyfully expected you, but in vain; I was in despair. At last when midnight came I sent my son to your lodging to enquire after you, but you may imagine my 'grief when I heard that nobody knew what had become of you. I passed a sleepless night, weeping all the time, and in the morning I went and complained to the police that you had taken off my daughter, and asked them to send after you and make you give her back to me. But only think, they laughed at me! 'Why did you let her go out without you? laughing in my face. 'Your daughter's in good hands,' says another, 'you know perfectly well where she is.' In fact I was grossly slandered."

"Slandered?" said the Corticelli.

"Yes, slandered, for it was as much as to say that I had consented to your being carried off, and if I had done that the fools might have known I would not have come to them about it. I went away in a rage to Dr. Vannini's, where I found your man, who told me that you had gone to Bologna, and that I could follow you if I liked. I consented to this plan, and I hope you wilt pay my travelling expenses. But I can't help telling you that this is rather beyond a joke."

I consoled her by telling her I would pay all she had spent, and we set off for Bologna the next day, and reached that town at an early hour. I sent my servants to the inn with my carriage, and I went to lodge with the Corticelli.

I spent a week with the girl, getting my meals from the inn, and enjoying a diversity of pleasures which I shall remember all my days; my young wanton had a large circle of female friends, all pretty and all kind. I lived with them like a sultan, and still I delight to recall this happy time, and I say with a sigh, 'Tempi passati'!

There are many towns in Italy where one can enjoy all the pleasures obtainable at Bologna; but nowhere so cheaply, so easily, or with so much freedom. The living is excellent, and there are arcades where one can walk in the shade in learned and witty company. It is a great pity that either from the air, the water, or the wine—for men of science have not made up their minds on the subject persons who live at Bologna are subject to a slight itch. The Bolognese, however, far from finding this unpleasant, seem to think it an advantage; it gives them the pleasure of scratching themselves. In springtime the ladies distinguish themselves by the grace with which they use their fingers.

Towards mid-Lent I left the Corticelli, wishing her a pleasant journey, for she was going to fulfil a year's engagement at Prague as second dancer. I promised to fetch her and her mother to Paris, and my readers will see how I kept my word.

I got to Modena the evening after I left Bologna, and I stopped there, with one of those sudden whims to which I have always been subject. Next morning I went out to see the pictures, and as I was returning to my lodging for dinner a blackguardly-looking fellow came up and ordered me, on the part of the Government, to continue my journey on the day following at latest.

"Very good," said I, and the fellow went away.

"Who is that man?" I said to the landlord.
"A SPY."

"A spy; and the Government dares to send such a fellow to me?"

"The 'borgello' must have sent him."

"Then the 'borgello' is the Governor of Modena—the infamous wretch!"

"Hush! hush! all the best families speak to him in the street."

"Then the best people are very low here, I suppose?"

"Not more than anywhere else. He is the manager of the opera house, and the greatest noblemen dine with him and thus secure his favour."

"It's incredible! But why should the high and mighty borgello send me away from Modena?"

"I don't know, but do you take my advice and go and speak to him; you will find him a fine fellow."

Instead of going to see this b. . . . I called on the Abbe Testa Grossa, whom I had known at Venice in 1753. Although he was a man of low extraction he had a keen wit. At this time he was old and resting on his laurels; he had fought his way into favour by the sheer force of merit, and his master, the Duke of Modena, had long chosen him as his representative with other powers.

Abbe Testa Grossa recognized me and gave me the most gracious reception, but when he heard of what had befallen me he seemed much annoyed.

"What can I do?" said I.

"You had better go, as the man may put a much more grievous insult on you."

"I will do so, but could you oblige me by telling me the reason for such a high-handed action?"

"Come again this evening; I shall probably be able to satisfy you."

I called on the abbe again in the evening, for I felt anxious to learn in what way I had offended the lord borgello, to whom I thought I was quite unknown. The abbe satisfied me.

"The borgello," said he, "saw your name on the bill which he receives daily containing a list of the names of those who enter or leave the city. He remembered that you were daring enough to escape from The Leads, and as he does not at all approve of that sort of thing he resolved not to let the Modenese be contaminated by so egregious an example of the defiance of justice, however unjust it may be; and in short he has given you the order to leave the town."

"I am much obliged, but I really wonder how it is that while you were telling me this you did not blush to be a subject of the Duke of Modena's. What an unworthy action! How contrary is such a system of government to all the best interests of the state!"

"You are quite right, my dear sir, but I am afraid that as yet men's eyes are not open to what best serves their interests."

"That is doubtless due to the fact that so many men are unworthy."

"I will not contradict you."

"Farewell, abbe."

"Farewell, M. Casanova."

Next morning, just as I was going to get into my carriage, a young man between twenty-five and thirty, tall and strong and broad shouldered, his eyes black and glittering, his eyebrows strongly arched, and his general air being that of a cut-throat, accosted me and begged me to step aside and hear what he had to say.

"If you like to stop at Parma for three days, and if you will promise to give me fifty sequins when I bring you the news that the borgello is dead, I promise to shoot him within the next twenty-four hours."

"Thanks. Such an animal as that should be allowed to die a natural death. Here's a crown to drink my health."

At the present time I feel very thankful that I acted as I did, but I confess that if I had felt sure that it was not a trap I should have promised the money. The fear of committing myself spared me this crime.

The next day I got to Parma, and I put up at the posting-house under the name of the Chevalier de Seingalt, which I still bear. When an honest man adopts a name which belongs to no one, no one has a right to contest his use of it; it becomes a man's duty to keep the name. I had now borne it for two years, but I often subjoined to it my family name.

When I got to Parma I dismissed Costa, but in a week after I had the misfortune to take him on again. His father, who was a poor violin player, as I had once been, with a large family to provide for, excited my pity.

I made enquiries about M. Antonio, but he had left the place; and M. Dubois Chalelereux, Director of the Mint, had gone to Venice with the permission of the Duke of Parma, to set up the beam, which was never brought into use. Republics are famous for their superstitious attachment to old customs; they are afraid that changes for the better may destroy the stability of the state, and the government of aristocratic Venice still preserves its original Greek character.

My Spaniard was delighted when I dismissed Costa and proportionately sorry when I took him back.

"He's no profligate," said Le Duc; "he is sober, and has no liking for bad company. But I think he's a robber, and a dangerous robber, too. I know it, because he seems so scrupulously careful not to cheat you in small things. Remember what I say, sir; he will do you. He is waiting to gain your confidence, and then he will strike home. Now, I am quite a different sort of fellow, a rogue in a small way; but you know me."

His insight was, keener than mine, for five or six months later the Italian robbed me of fifty thousand crowns. Twenty-three years afterwards, in 1784, I found him in Venice, valet to Count Hardegg, and I felt inclined to have him hanged. I shewed him by proof positive that I could do so if I liked; but he had resource to tears and supplications, and to the intercession of a worthy man named Bertrand, who lived with the ambassador of the King of Sardinia. I esteemed this individual, and he appealed to me successfully to pardon Costa. I asked the wretch what he had done with the gold and jewels he had stolen from me, and he told me that he had lost the whole of it in furnishing funds for a bank at Biribi, that he had been despoiled by his own associates, and had been poor and miserable ever since.

In the same year in which he robbed me he married Momolo's daughter, and after making her a mother he abandoned her.

To pursue our story.

At Turin I lodged in a private house with the Abbe Gama, who had been expecting me. In spite of the good abbe's sermon on economy, I took the whole of the first floor, and a fine suite it was.

We discussed diplomatic topics, and he assured me that I should be accredited in May, and that he would give me instructions as to the part I was to play. I was pleased with his commission, and I told the abbe that I should be ready to go to Augsburg whenever the ambassadors of the belligerent powers met there.

After making the necessary arrangements with my landlady with regard to my meals I went to a coffeehouse to read the papers, and the first person I saw was the Marquis Desarmoises, whom I had known in Savoy. The first thing he said was that all games of chance were forbidden, and that the ladies I had met would no doubt be delighted to see me. As for himself, he said that he lived by playing backgammon, though he was not at all lucky at it, as talent went for more than luck at that game. I can understand how, if fortune is neutral, the best player will win, but I do not see how the contrary can take place.

We went for a walk in the promenade leading to the citadel, where I saw numerous extremely pretty women. In Turin the fair sex is most delightful, but the police regulations are troublesome to a degree. Owing to the town being a small one and thinly peopled, the police spies find out everything. Thus one cannot enjoy any little freedoms without great precautions and the aid of cunning procuresses, who have to be well paid, as they would be cruelly punished if they were found out. No prostitutes and no kept women are allowed, much to the delight of the married women, and with results which the ignorant police might have anticipated. As well be imagined, pederasty has a fine field in this town, where the passions are kept under lock and key.

Amongst the beauties I looked at, one only attracted me. I asked Desarmoises her name, as he knew all of them.

"That's the famous Leah," said he; "she is a Jewess, and impregnable. She has resisted the attacks of the best strategists in Turin. Her father's a famous horse-dealer; you can go and see her easily enough, but there's nothing to be done there."

The greater the difficulty the more I felt spurred on to attempt it.

"Take me there," said I, to Desarmoises.

"As soon as you please."

I asked him to dine with me, and we were on our way when we met M. Zeroli and two or three other persons whom I had met at Aix. I gave and received plenty of compliments, but not wishing to pay them any visits I excused myself on the pretext of business.

When we had finished dinner Desarmoises took me to the horse-dealer's. I asked if he had a good saddle horse. He called a lad and gave his orders, and whilst he was speaking the charming daughter appeared on the scene. She was dazzlingly beautiful, and could not be more than twenty-two. Her figure was as lissom as a nymph's, her hair a raven black, her complexion a meeting of the lily and the rose, her eyes full of fire, her lashes long, and her eye-brows so well arched that they seemed ready to make war on any who would dare the conquest of her charms. All about her betokened an educated mind and knowledge of the world.

I was so absorbed in the contemplation of her charms that I did not notice the horse when it was brought to me. However, I proceeded to scrutinise it, pretending to be an expert, and after feeling the knees and legs, turning back the ears, and looking at the teeth, I tested its behaviour at a walk, a trot, and a gallop, and then told the Jew that I would come and try it myself in top-boots the next day. The horse was a fine dappled bay, and was priced at forty Piedmontese pistoles—about a hundred sequins.

"He is gentleness itself," said Leah, "and he ambles as fast as any other horse trots."

"You have ridden it, then?"

"Often, sir, and if I were rich I would never sell him."

"I won't buy the horse till I have seen you ride it."

She blushed at this.

"You must oblige the gentleman," said her father. She consented to do so, and I promised to come again at nine o'clock the next day.

I was exact to time, as may be imagined, and I found Leah in riding costume. What proportions! What a Venus Callipyge! I was captivated.

Two horses were ready, and she leapt on hers with the ease and grace of a practised rider, and I got up on my horse. We rode together for some distance. The horse went well enough, but what of that; all my eyes were for her.

As we were turning, I said,—

"Fair Leah, I will buy the horse, but as a present for you; and if you will not take it I shall leave Turin today. The only condition I attach to the gift is, that you will ride with me whenever I ask you."

I saw she seemed favourably inclined to my proposal, so I told her that I should stay six weeks at Turin, that I had fallen in love with her on the promenade, and that the purchase of the horse had been a mere pretext for discovering to her my feelings. She replied modestly that she was vastly flattered by the liking I had taken to her, and that I need not have made her such a present to assure myself of her friendship.

"The condition you impose on me is an extremely pleasant one, and I am sure that my father will like me to accept it."

To this she added,—

"All I ask is for you to make me the present before him, repeating that you will only buy it on the condition that I will accept it."

I found the way smoother than I had expected, and I did what she asked me. Her father, whose name was Moses, thought it a good bargain, congratulated his daughter, took the forty pistoles and gave me a receipt, and begged me to do them the honour of breakfasting with them the next day. This was just what I wanted.

The following morning Moses received me with great respect. Leah, who was in her ordinary clothes, told me that if I liked to ride she would put on her riding habit.

"Another day," said I; "to-day I should like to converse with you in your own house."

But the father, who was as greedy as most Jews are, said that if I liked driving he could sell me a pretty phaeton with two excellent horses.

"You must shew them to the gentleman," said Leah, possibly in concert with her father.

Moses said nothing, but went out to get the horses harnessed.

"I will look at them," I said to Leah, "but I won't buy, as I should not know what to do with them."

"You can take your lady-love out for a drive."

"That would be you; but perhaps you would be afraid!"

"Not at all, if you drove in the country or the suburbs."

"Very good, Leah, then I will look at them."

The father came in, and we went downstairs. I liked the carriage and the horses, and I told Leah so.

"Well," said Moses, "you can have them now for four hundred sequins, but after Easter the price will be five hundred sequins at least."

Leah got into the carriage, and I sat beside her, and we went for an hour's drive into the country. I told Moses I would give him an answer by the next day, and he went about his business, while Leah and I went upstairs again.

"It's quite worth four hundred sequins," said I, "and to-morrow I will buy it with pleasure; but on the same condition as that on which I bought the horse, and something more—namely, that you will grant me all the favours that a tender lover can desire."

"You speak plainly, and I will answer you in the same way. I'm an honest girl, sir, and not for sale."

"All women, dear Leah, whether they are honest or not, are for sale. When a man has plenty of time he buys the woman his heart desires by unremitting attentions; but when he's in a hurry he buys her with presents, and even with money."

"Then he's a clumsy fellow; he would do better to let sentiment and attention plead his cause and gain the victory."

"I wish I could give myself that happiness, fair Leah, but I'm in a great hurry."

As I finished this sentence her father came in, and I left the house telling him that if I could not come the next day I would come the day after, and that we could talk about the phaeton then.

It was plain that Leah thought I was lavish of my money, and would make a capital dupe. She would relish the phaeton, as she had relished the horse, but I knew that I was not quite such a fool as that. It had not cost me much trouble to resolve to chance the loss of a hundred sequins, but beyond that I wanted some value for my money.

I temporarily suspended my visits to see how Leah and her father would settle it amongst themselves. I reckoned on the Jew's greediness to work well for me. He was very fond of money, and must have been angry that his daughter had not made me buy the phaeton by some means or another, for so long as the phaeton was bought the rest would be perfectly indifferent to him. I felt almost certain that they would come and see me.

The following Saturday I saw the fair Jewess on the promenade. We were near enough for me to accost her without seeming to be anxious to do so, and her look seemed to say, "Come."

"We see no more of you now," said she, "but come and breakfast with me to-morrow, or I will send you back the horse."

I promised to be with her in good time, and, as the reader will imagine,
I kept my word.

The breakfast party was almost confined to ourselves, for though her aunt was present she was only there for decency's sake. After breakfast we resolved to have a ride, and she changed her clothes before me, but also before her aunt. She first put on her leather breeches, then let her skirts fall, took off her corset, and donned a jacket. With seeming indifference I succeeded in catching a glimpse of a magnificent breast; but the sly puss knew how much my indifference was worth.

"Will you arrange my frill?" said she.

This was a warm occupation for me, and I am afraid my hand was indiscreet. Nevertheless, I thought I detected a fixed design under all this seeming complaisance, and I was on my guard.

Her father came up just as we were getting on horseback.

"If you will buy the phaeton and horses," said he, "I will abate twenty sequins."

"All that depends on your daughter," said I.

We set off at a walk, and Leah told me that she had been imprudent enough to confess to her father that she could make me buy the carriage, and that if I did not wish to embroil her with him I would be kind enough to purchase it.

"Strike the bargain," said she, "and you can give it me when you are sure of my love."

"My dear Leah, I am your humble servant, but you know on what condition."

"I promise to drive out with you whenever you please, without getting out of the carriage, but I know you would not care for that. No, your affection was only a temporary caprice."

"To convince you of the contrary I will buy the phaeton and put it in a coach-house. I will see that the horses are taken-care of, though I shall not use them. But if you do not make me happy in the course of a week I shall re-sell the whole."

"Come to us to-morrow."

"I will do so, but I trust have some pledge of your affection this morning."

"This morning? It's impossible."

"Excuse me; I will go upstairs with you, and you can shew me more than one kindness while you are undressing."

We came back, and I was astonished to hear her telling her father that the phaeton was mine, and all he had to do was to put in the horses. The Jew grinned, and we all went upstairs, and Leah coolly said,—

"Count out the money."

"I have not any money about me, but I will write you a cheque, if you like."

"Here is paper."

I wrote a cheque on Zappata for three hundred sequins, payable at sight. The Jew went off to get the money, and Leah remained alone with me.

"You have trusted me," she said, "and have thus shewn yourself worthy of my love."

"Then undress, quick!"

"No, my aunt is about the house; and as I cannot shut the door without exciting suspicion, she might come in; but I promise that you shall be content with me tomorrow. Nevertheless, I am going to undress, but you must go in this closet; you may come back when I have got my woman's clothes on again."

I agreed to this arrangement, and she shut me in. I examined the door, and discovered a small chink between the boards. I got on a stool, and saw Leah sitting on a sofa opposite to me engaged in undressing herself. She took off her shift and wiped her breasts and her feet with a towel, and just as she had taken off her breeches, and was as naked as my hand, one of her rings happened to slip off her finger, and rolled under the sofa. She got up, looked to right and left, and then stooped to search under the sofa, and to do this she had to kneel with her head down. When she got back to couch, the towel came again into requisition, and she wiped herself all over in such a manner that all her charms were revealed to my eager eyes. I felt sure that she knew I was a witness of all these operations, and she probably guessed what a fire the sight would kindle in my inflammable breast.

At last her toilette was finished, and she let me out. I clasped her in my arms, with the words, "I have seen everything." She pretended not to believe me, so I chewed her the chink, and was going to obtain my just dues, when the accursed Moses came in. He must have been blind or he would have seen the state his daughter had put me in; however, he thanked me, and gave me a receipt for the money, saying, "Everything in my poor house is at your service."

I bade them adieu, and I went away in an ill temper. I got into my phaeton, and drove home and told the coachman to find me a stable for the horses and a coach-house for the carriage.

I did not expect to see Leah again, and I felt enraged with her. She had pleased me only too much by her voluptuous attitudes, but she had set up an irritation wholly hostile to Love. She had made Love a robber, and the hungry boy had consented, but afterwards, when he craved more substantial fare, she refused him, and ardour was succeeded by contempt. Leah did not want to confess herself to be what she really was, and my love would not declare itself knavish.

I made the acquaintance of an amiable chevalier, a soldier, a man of letters, and a great lover of horses, who introduced me to several pleasant families. However, I did not cultivate them, as they only offered me the pleasures of sentiment, while I longed for lustier fare for which I was willing to pay heavily. The Chevalier de Breze was not the man for me; he was too respectable for a profligate like myself. He bought the phaeton and horses, and I only lost thirty sequins by the transaction.

A certain M. Baretti, who had known me at Aix, and had been the Marquis de Pries croupier, took me to see the Mazzoli, formerly a dancer, and then mistress to the Chevalier Raiberti, a hardheaded but honest man, who was then secretary for foreign affairs. Although the Mazzoli was by no means pretty, she was extremely complaisant, and had several girls at her house for me to see; but I did not think any of them worthy of occupying Leah's place. I fancied I no longer loved Leah, but I was wrong.

The Chevalier Cocona, who had the misfortune to be suffering from a venereal disease, gave me up his mistress, a pretty little 'soubrette'; but in spite of the evidence of my own eyes, and in spite of the assurances she gave me, I could not make up my mind to have her, and my fear made me leave her untouched. Count Trana, a brother of the chevalier's whom I had known at Aix, introduced me to Madame de Sc——, a lady of high rank and very good-looking, but she tried to involve me in a criminal transaction, and I ceased to call on her. Shortly after, Count Trana's uncle died and he became rich and got married, but he lived an unhappy life.

I was getting bored, and Desarmoises, who had all his meals with me, did not know what to do. At last he advised me to make the acquaintance of a certain Madame R——, a Frenchwoman, and well known in Turin as a milliner and dressmaker. She had six or eight girls working for her in a room adjoining her shop. Desarmoises thought that if I got in there I might possibly be able to find one to my taste. As my purse was well furnished I thought I should not have much difficulty, so I called on Madame R——. I was agreeably surprised to find Leah there, bargaining for a quantity of articles, all of which she pronounced to be too dear. She told me kindly but reproachfully that she had thought I must be ill.

"I have been very busy," I said; and felt all my old ardour revive. She asked me to come to a Jewish wedding, where there would be a good many people and several pretty girls. I knew that ceremonies of this kind are very amusing, and I promised to be present. She proceeded with her bargaining, but the price was still too high and she left the shop. Madame R—— was going to put back all the trifles in their places, but I said,—

"I will take the lot myself."

She smiled, and I drew out my purse and paid the money.

"Where do you live, sir?" said she; "and when shall I send you your purchases?"

"You may bring them to-morrow yourself, and do me the honour of breakfasting with me."

"I can never leave the shop, sir." In spite of her thirty-five years, Madame R—— was still what would be called a tasty morsel, and she had taken my fancy.

"I want some dark lace," said I.

"Then kindly follow me, sir."

I was delighted when I entered the room to see a lot of young work-girls, all charming, hard at work, and scarcely daring to look at me. Madame R—— opened several cupboards, and showed me some magnificent lace. I was distracted by the sight of so many delicious nymphs, and I told her that I wanted the lace for two 'baoutes' in the Venetian style. She knew what I meant. The lace cost me upwards of a hundred sequins. Madame R—— told two of her girls to bring me the lace the next day, together with the goods which Leah had thought too dear. They meekly replied,—

"Yes, mother."

They rose and kissed the mother's hand, which I thought a ridiculous ceremony; however, it gave me an opportunity of examining them, and I thought them delicious. We went back to the shop, and sitting down by the counter I enlarged on the beauty of the girls, adding, though not with strict truth, that I vastly preferred their mistress. She thanked me for the compliment and told me plainly that she had a lover, and soon after named him. He was the Comte de St. Giles, an infirm and elderly man, and by no means a model lover. I thought Madame R—— was jesting, but next day I ascertained that she was speaking the truth. Well, everyone to his taste, and I suspect that she was more in love with the count's purse than his person. I had met him at the "Exchange" coffeehouse.

The next day the two pretty milliners brought me my goods. I offered them chocolate, but they firmly and persistently declined. The fancy took me to send them to Leah with all the things she had chosen, and I bade them return and tell me what sort of a reception they had had. They said they would do so, and waited for me to write her a note.

I could not give them the slightest mark of affection. I dared not shut the door, and the mistress and the ugly young woman of the house kept going and coming all the time; but when they came back I waited for them on the stairs, and giving them a sequin each told each of them that she might command my heart if she would. Leah had accepted my handsome present and sent to say that she was waiting for me.

As I was walking aimlessly about in the afternoon I happened to pass the milliner's shop, and Madame R—— saw me and made me come in and sit down beside her.

"I am really much obliged to you," said she, "for your kindness to my girls. They came home enchanted. Tell me frankly whether you are really in love with the pretty Jewess."

"I am really in love with her, but as she will not make me happy I have signed my own dismissal."

"You were quite right. All Leah thinks of is duping those who are captivated by her charms."

"Do not your charming apprentices follow your maxims?"

"No; but they are only complaisant when I give them leave."

"Then I commend myself to your intercession, for they would not even take a cup of chocolate from me."

"They were perfectly right not to accept your chocolate: but I see you do not know the ways of Turin. Do you find yourself comfortable in your present lodging?"

"Quite so."

"Are you perfectly free to do what you like?"

"I think so."

"Can you give supper to anyone you like in your own rooms? I am certain you can't."

"I have not had the opportunity of trying the experiment so far, but I believe . . . ."

"Don't flatter yourself by believing anything; that house is full of the spies of the police."

"Then you think that I could not give you and two or three of your girls a little supper?"

"I should take very good care not to go to it, that's all I know. By next morning it would be known to all the town, and especially to the police."

"Well, supposing I look out for another lodging?"

"It's the same everywhere. Turin is a perfect nest of spies; but I do know a house where you could live at ease, and where my girls might perhaps be able to bring you your purchases. But we should have to be very careful."

"Where is the house I will be guided by you in everything."

"Don't trust a Piedmontese; that's the first commandment here."

She then gave me the address of a small furnished house, which was only inhabited by an old door-keeper and his wife.

"They will let it you by the month," said she, "and if you pay a month in advance you need not even tell them your name."

I found the house to be a very pretty one, standing in a lonely street at about two hundred paces from the citadel. One gate, large enough to admit a carriage, led into the country. I found everything to be as Madame R—— had described it. I paid a month in advance without any bargaining, and in a day I had settled in my new lodging. Madame R—— admired my celerity.

I went to the Jewish wedding and enjoyed myself, for there is something at once solemn and ridiculous about the ceremony; but I resisted all Leah's endeavours to get me once more into her meshes.. I hired a close carriage from her father, which with the horses I placed in the coach-house and stables of my new house. Thus I was absolutely free to go whenever I would by night or by day, for I was at once in the town and in the country. I was obliged to tell the inquisitive Gama where I was living, and I hid nothing from Desarmoises, whose needs made him altogether dependent on me. Nevertheless I gave orders that my door was shut to them as to everyone else, unless I had given special instructions that they were to be admitted. I had no reason to doubt the fidelity of my two servants.

In this blissful abode I enjoyed all Mdlle. R——'s girls, one after the other. The one I wanted always brought a companion, whom I usually sent back after giving her a slice of the cake. The last of them, whose name was Victorine, as fair as day and as soft as a dove, had the misfortune to be tied, though she knew nothing about it. Mdlle. R——, who was equally ignorant on the subject, had represented her to me as a virgin, and so I thought her for two long hours in which I strove with might and main to break the charm, or rather open the shell. All my efforts were in vain. I was exhausted at last, and I wanted to see in what the obstacle consisted. I put her in the proper position, and armed with a candle I began my scrutiny. I found a fleshy membrane pierced by so small a hole that large pin's head could scarcely have gone through. Victorine encouraged me to force a passage with my little finger, but in vain I tried to pierce this wall, which nature had made impassable by all ordinary means. I was tempted to see what I could do with a bistoury, and the girl wanted me to try, but I was afraid of the haemorrhage which might have been dangerous, and I wisely refrained.

Poor Victorine, condemned to die a maid, unless some clever surgeon performed the same operation that was undergone by Mdlle. Cheruffini shortly after M. Lepri married her, wept when I said,—

"My dear child, your little Hymen defies the most vigorous lover to enter his temple."

But I consoled her by saying that a good surgeon could easily make a perfect woman of her.

In the morning I told Madame R—— of the case.

She laughed and said,—

"It may prove a happy accident for Victorine; it may make her fortune."

A few years after the Count of Padua had her operated on, and made her fortune. When I came back from Spain I found that she was with child, so that I could not exact the due reward for all the trouble I had taken with her.

Early in the morning on Maunday Thursday they told me that Moses and Leah wanted to see me. I had not expected to see them, but I welcomed them warmly. Throughout Holy Week the Jews dared not shew themselves in the streets of Turin, and I advised them to stay with me till the Saturday. Moses began to try and get me to purchase a ring from him, and I judged from that that I should not have to press them very much.

"I can only buy this ring from Leah's hands," said I.

He grinned, thinking doubtless that I intended to make her a present of it, but I was resolved to disappoint him. I gave them a magnificent dinner and supper, and in the evening they were shewn a double-bedded room not far from mine. I might have put them in different rooms, and Leah in a room adjoining mine, which would have facilitated any nocturnal excursions; but after all I had done for her I was resolved to owe nothing to a surprise; she should come of herself.

The next day Moses (who noticed that I had not yet bought the ring) was obliged to go out on business, and asked for the loan of my carriage for the whole day, telling me that he would come for his daughter in the evening. I had the horses harnessed, and when he was gone I bought the ring for six hundred sequins, but on my own terms. I was in my own house, and Leah could not deceive me. As soon as the father was safely out of the way I possessed myself of the daughter. She proved a docile and amorous subject the whole day. I had reduced her to a state of nature, and though her body was as perfect as can well be imagined I used it and abused it in every way imaginable. In the evening her father found her looking rather tired, but he seemed as pleased as I was. Leah was not quite so well satisfied, for till the moment of their departure she was expecting me to give her the ring, but I contented myself with saying that I should like to reserve myself the pleasure of taking it to her.

On Easter Monday a man brought me a note summoning me to appear at the police office.

CHAPTER XII

My Victory Over the Deputy Chief of Police—My Departure—Chamberi—Desarmoises's Daughter—M. Morin—M * * M * * *—At Aix—The Young Boarder—Lyons—Paris

This citation, which did not promise to lead to anything agreeable, surprised and displeased me exceedingly. However, I could not avoid it, so I drove to the office of the deputy-superintendent of police. I found him sitting at a long table, surrounded by about a score of people in a standing posture. He was a man of sixty, hideously ugly, his enormous nose half destroyed by an ulcer hidden by a large black silk plaster, his mouth of huge dimensions, his lips thick, with small green eyes and eyebrows which had partly turned white. As soon as this disgusting fellow saw me, he began,—

"You are the Chevalier de Seingalt?"

"That is my name, and I have come here to ask how I can oblige you?"

"I have summoned you here to order you to leave the place in three days at latest."

"And as you have no right to give such an order, I have come here to tell you that I shall go when I please, and not before."

"I will expel you by force."

"You may do that whenever you please. I cannot resist force, but I trust you will give the matter a second thought; for in a well-ordered city they do not expel a man who has committed no crimes, and has a balance of a hundred thousand francs at the bank."

"Very good, but in three days you have plenty of time to pack up and arrange matters with your banker. I advise you to obey, as the command comes from the king."

"If I were to leave the town I should become accessory to your injustice! I will not obey, but since you mention the king's name, I will go to his majesty at once, and he will deny your words or revoke the unjust order you have given me with such publicity."

"Pray, does not the king possess the power to make you go?"

"Yes, by force, but not by justice. He has also the power to kill me, but he would have to provide the executioner, as he could not make me commit suicide."

"You argue well, but nevertheless you will obey."

"I argue well, but I did not learn the art from you, and I will not obey."

With these words I turned my back on him, and left without another word.

I was in a furious rage. I felt inclined to offer overt resistance to all the myrmidons of the infamous superintendent. Nevertheless I soon calmed myself, and summoning prudence to my aid I remembered the Chevalier Raiberti, whom I had seen at his mistress's house, and I decided on asking his advice. He was the chief permanent official in the department of foreign affairs. I told the coachman to drive to his house, and I recounted to him the whole tale, saying, finally, that I should like to speak to the king, as I was resolved that I would not go unless I was forced to do so. The worthy man advised me to go to the Chevalier Osorio, the principal secretary for foreign affairs, who could always get an audience of the king. I was pleased with his advice, and I went immediately to the minister, who was a Sicilian and a man of parts. He gave me a very good reception, and after I had informed him of the circumstances of the case I begged him to communicate the matter to his majesty, adding that as the superintendent's order appeared horribly unjust to me I was resolved not to obey it unless compelled to do so by main force. He promised to oblige me in the way I wished, and told me to call again the next day.

After leaving him I took a short walk to cool myself, and then went to the Abbe Gama, hoping to be the first to impart my ridiculous adventure to him. I was disappointed; he already knew that I had been ordered to go, and how I had answered the superintendent. When he saw that I persisted in my determination to resist, he did not condemn my firmness, though he must have thought it very extraordinary, for the good abbe could not understand anybody's disobeying the order of the authorities. He assured me that if I had to go he would send me the necessary instructions to any address I liked to name.

The next day the Chevalier Osorio received me with the utmost politeness, which I thought a good omen. The Chevalier Raiberti had spoken to him in my behalf, and he had laid the matter before the king and also before the Count d'Aglie, and the result was that

I could stay as long as I liked. The Count d'Aglie was none other than the horrible superintendent. I was told that I must wait on him, and he would give me leave to remain at Turin till my affairs were settled.

"My only business here," said I, "is to spend my money till I have instructions from the Court of Portugal to attend the Congress of Augsburg on behalf of his most faithful majesty."

"Then you think that this Congress will take place?"

"Nobody doubts it."

"Somebody believes it will all end in smoke. However, I am delighted to have been of service to you, and I shall be curious to hear what sort of reception you get from the superintendent."

I felt ill at ease. I went to the police office immediately, glad to shew myself victorious, and anxious to see how the superintendent would look when I came in. However, I could not flatter myself that he looked ashamed of himself; these people have a brazen forehead, and do not know what it is to blush.

As soon as he saw me, he began,—

"The Chevalier Osorio tells me that you have business in Turin which will keep you for some days. You may therefore stay, but you must tell me as nearly as possible how long a time you require."

"I cannot possibly tell you that."

"Why? if you don't mind telling me."

"I am awaiting instructions from the Court of Portugal to attend the Congress to be held at Augsburg, and before I could tell you how long I shall have to stay I should be compelled to ask his most faithful majesty. If this time is not sufficient for me to do my business, I will intimate the fact to you."

"I shall be much obliged by your doing so."

This time I made him a bow, which was returned, and on leaving the office I returned to the Chevalier Osorio, who said, with a smile, that I had caught the superintendent, as I had taken an indefinite period, which left me quite at my ease.

The diplomatic Gama, who firmly believed that the Congress would meet, was delighted when I told him that the Chevalier Osorio was incredulous on the subject. He was charmed to think his wit keener than the minister's; it exalted him in his own eyes. I told him that whatever the chevalier might say I would go to Augsburg, and that I would set out in three or four weeks.

Madame R. congratulated me over and over again, for she was enchanted that I had humiliated the superintendent; but all the same we thought we had better give up our little suppers. As I had had a taste of all her girls, this was not such a great sacrifice for me to make.

I continued thus till the middle of May, when I left Turin, after receiving letters from the Abbe Gama to Lord Stormont, who was to represent England at the approaching Congress. It was with this nobleman that I was to work in concert at the Congress.

Before going to Germany I wanted to see Madame d'Urfe, and I wrote to her, asking her to send me a letter of introduction to M. de Rochebaron, who might be useful to me. I also asked M. Raiberti to give me a letter for Chamberi, where I wanted to visit the divine M—— M—— (of whom I still thought with affection) at her convent grating. I wrote to my friend Valenglard, asking him to remind Madame Morin that she had promised to shew me a likeness to somebody at Chamberi.

But here I must note down an event worthy of being recorded, which was extremely prejudicial to me.

Five or six days before my departure Desarmoises came to me looking very downcast, and told me that he had been ordered to leave Turin in twenty-four hours.

"Do you know why?" I asked him.

"Last night when I was at the coffee-house, Count Scarnafis dared to say that France subsidised the Berne newspapers. I told him he lied, at which he rose and left the place in a rage, giving me a glance the meaning of which is not doubtful. I followed him to bring him to reason or to give him satisfaction; but he would do nothing and I suspect he went to the police to complain. I shall have to leave Turin early to-morrow morning."

"You're a Frenchman, and as you can claim the protection of your ambassador you will be wrong to leave so suddenly."

"In the first place the ambassador is away, and in the second my cruel father disavows me. No, I would rather go, and wait for you at Lyons. All I want is for you to lend me a hundred crowns, for which I will give you an account."

"It will be an easy account to keep," said I, "but a long time before it is settled."

"Possibly; but if it is in my power I will shew my gratitude for the kindnesses you have done me."

I gave him a hundred crowns and wished him a pleasant journey, telling him that I should stop some time at Lyons.

I got a letter of credit on an Augsburg house, and three days after I left Turin I was at Chamberi. There was only one inn there in those days, so I was not much puzzled to choose where I would go, but for all that I found myself very comfortable.

As I entered my room, I was struck by seeing an extremely pretty girl coming out of an adjacent room.

"Who is that young lady?" said I to the chambermaid who was escorting me.

"That's the wife of a young gentleman who has to keep his bed to get cured of a sword-thrust which he received four days ago on his way from France."

I could not look at her without feeling the sting of concupiscence. As I was leaving my room I saw the door half open, and I stopped short and offered my services as a neighbour. She thanked me politely, and asked me in. I saw a handsome young man sitting up in bed, so I went up to enquire how he felt.

"The doctor will not let him talk," said the young lady, "on account of a sword-thrust in the chest he received at half a league from here. We hope he will be all right in a few days, and then we can continue our journey."

"Where are you going, madam?"

"To Geneva."

Just as I was leaving, a maid came to ask me if I would take supper in my own room or with the lady. I laughed at her stupidity, and said I would sup in my own apartment, adding that I had not the honour of the lady's acquaintance.

At this the young lady said it would give her great pleasure if I would sup with her, and the husband repeated this assurance in a whisper. I accepted the invitation gratefully, and I thought that they were really pleased. The lady escorted me out as far as the stairs, and I took the liberty of kissing her hand, which in France is a declaration of tender though respectful affection.

At the post-office I found a letter from Valenglard, telling me that Madame Morin would wait on me at Chamberi if I would send her a carriage, and another from Desarmoises dated from Lyons. He told me that as he was on his way from Chamberi he had encountered his daughter in company with a rascal who had carried her off. He had buried his sword in his body, and would have killed them if he had been able to stop their carriage. He suspected that they had been staying in Chamberi, and he begged me to try and persuade his daughter to return to Lyons; and he added that if she would not do so I ought to oblige him by sending her back by force. He assured me that they were not married, and he begged me to answer his letter by express, for which purpose he sent me his address.

I guessed at once that this daughter of his was my fair neighbour, but I did not feel at all inclined to come to the aid of the father in the way he wished.

As soon as I got back to the inn I sent off Le Duc in a travelling carriage to Madame Morin, whom I informed by letter that as I was only at Chamberi for her sake I would await her convenience. This done, I abandoned myself to the delight I felt at the romantic adventure which fortune had put in my way.

I repeated Mdlle. Desarmoises and her ravisher, and I did not care to enquire whether I was impelled in what I did by virtue or vice; but I could not help perceiving that my motives were of a mixed nature; for if I were amorous, I was also very glad to be of assistance to two young lovers, and all the more from my knowledge of the father's criminal passion.

On entering their room I found the invalid in the surgeon's hands. He pronounced the wound not to be dangerous, in spite of its depth; suppuration had taken place without setting up inflammation—in short, the young man only wanted time and rest. When the doctor had gone I congratulated the patient on his condition, advising him to be careful what he ate, and to keep silent. I then gave Mdlle. Desarmoises her father's letter, and I said farewell for the present, telling them that I would go to my own room till supper-time. I felt sure that she would come and speak to me after reading her father's letter.

In a quarter of an hour she knocked timidly at my door, and when I let her in she gave me back the letter and asked me what I thought of doing.

"Nothing. I shall be only too happy, however, if I can be of any service to you."

"Ah! I breathe again!"

"Could you imagine me pursuing any other line of conduct? I am much interested in you, and will do all in my power to help you. Are you married?"

"Not yet, but we are going to be married when we get to Geneva."

"Sit down and tell me all about yourself. I know that your father is unhappily in love with you, and that you avoid his attentions."

"He has told you that much? I am glad of it. A year ago he came to Lyons, and as soon as I knew he was in the town I took refuge with a friend of my mother's, for I was aware that I could not stay in the same house with my father for an hour without exposing myself to the most horrible outrage. The young man in bed is the son of a rich Geneva merchant. My father introduced him to me two years ago, and we soon fell in love with each other. My father went away to Marseilles, and my lover asked my mother to give me in marriage to him; but she did not feel authorized to do so without my father's consent. She wrote and asked him, but he replied that he would announce his decision when he returned to Lyons. My lover went to Geneva, and as his father approved of the match he returned with all the necessary documents and a strong letter of commendation from M. Tolosan. When my father came to Lyons I escaped, as I told you, and my lover got M. Tolosan to ask my hand for him of my father. His reply was, 'I can give no answer till she returns to my house!'

"M. Tolosan brought this reply to me, and I told him that I was ready to obey if my mother would guarantee my safety. She replied, however, that she knew her husband too well to dare to have us both under the same roof. Again did M. Tolosan endeavour to obtain my father's consent, but to no purpose. A few days after he left Lyons, telling us that he was first going to Aix and then to Turin, and as it was evident that he would never give his consent my lover proposed that I should go off with him, promising to marry me as soon as we reached Geneva. By ill luck we travelled through Savoy, and thus met my father. As soon as he saw us he stopped the carriage and called to me to get out. I began to shriek, and my lover taking me in his arms to protect me my father stabbed him in the chest. No doubt he would have killed him, but seeing that my shrieks were bringing people to our rescue, and probably believing that my lover was as good as dead, he got on horseback again and rode off at full speed. I can chew you the sword still covered with blood."

"I am obliged to answer this letter of his, and I am thinking how I can obtain his consent."

"That's of no consequence; we can marry and be happy without it."

"True, but you ought not to despise your dower."

"Good heavens! what dower? He has no money!"

"But on the death of his father, the Marquis Desarmoises . . . ."

"That's all a lie. My father has only a small yearly pension for having served thirty years as a Government messenger. His father has been dead these thirty years, and my mother and my sister only live by the work they do."

I was thunderstruck at the impudence of the fellow, who, after imposing on me so long, had himself put me in a position to discover his deceit. I said nothing. Just then we were told that supper was ready, and we sat at table for three hours talking the matter over. The poor wounded man had only to listen to me to know my feelings on the subject. His young mistress, as witty as she was pretty, jested on the foolish passion of her father, who had loved her madly ever since she was eleven.

"And you were always able to resist his attempts?" said I.

"Yes, whenever he pushed things too far."

"And how long did this state of things continue?"

"For two years. When I was thirteen he thought I was ripe, and tried to gather the fruit; but I began to shriek, and escaped from his bed stark naked, and I went to take refuge with my mother, who from that day forth would not let me sleep with him again."

"You used to sleep with him? How could your mother allow it?"

"She never thought that there was anything criminal in his affection for me, and I knew nothing about it. I thought that what he did to me, and what he made me do to him, were mere trifles."

"But you have saved the little treasure?"

"I have kept it for my lover."

The poor lover, who was suffering more from the effects of hunger than from his wounds, laughed at this speech of hers, and she ran to him and covered his face with kisses. All this excited me intensely. Her story had been told with too much simplicity not to move me, especially when I had her before my eyes, for she possessed all the attractions which a woman can have, and I almost forgave her father for forgetting she was his daughter and falling in love with her.

When she escorted me back to my room I made her feel my emotion, and she began to laugh; but as my servants were close by I was obliged to let her go.

Early next morning I wrote to her father that his daughter had resolved not to leave her lover, who was only slightly wounded, that they were in perfect safety and under the protection of the law at Chamberi, and finally that having heard their story, and judging them to be well matched, I could only approve of the course they had taken. When I had finished I went into their room and gave them the letter to read, and seeing the fair runaway at a loss how to express her 'gratitude, I begged the invalid to let me kiss her.

"Begin with me," said he, opening his arms.

My hypocritical love masked itself under the guise of paternal affection. I embraced the lover, and then more amorously I performed the same office for the mistress, and skewed them my purse full of gold, telling them it was at their service. While this was going on the surgeon came in, and I retired to my room.

At eleven o'clock Madame Morin and her daughter arrived, preceded by Le Duc on horseback, who announced their approach by numerous smacks of his whip. I welcomed her with open arms, thanking her for obliging me.

The first piece of news she gave me was that Mdlle. Roman had become mistress to Louis XV., that she lived in a beautiful house at Passi, and that she was five months gone with child. Thus she was in a fair way to become queen of France, as my divine oracle had predicted.

"At Grenoble," she added, "you are the sole topic of conversation; and I advise you not to go there unless you wish to settle in the country, for they would never let you go. You would have all the nobility at your feet, and above all, the ladies anxious to know the lot of their daughters. Everybody believes in judicial astrology now, and Valenglard triumphs. He has bet a hundred Louis to fifty that my niece will be delivered of a young prince, and he is certain of winning; though to be sure, if he loses, everybody will laugh at him."

"Don't be afraid of his losing."

"Is it quite certain?"

"Has not the horoscope proved truthful in the principal particular? If the other circumstances do not follow, I must have made a great mistake in my calculations."

"I am delighted to hear you say so."

"I am going to Paris and I hope you will give me a letter of introduction to Madame Varnier, so that I may have the pleasure of seeing your niece."

"You shall have the letter to-morrow without fail."

I introduced Mdlle. Desarmoises to her under the family name of her lover, and invited her to dine with Madame Morin and myself. After dinner we went to the convent, and M—— M—— came down very surprised at this unexpected visit from her aunt; but when she saw me she had need of all her presence of mind. When her aunt introduced me to her by name, she observed with true feminine tact that during her stay at Aix she had seen me five or six times at the fountain, but that I could not remember her features as she had always worn her veil. I admired her wit as much as her exquisite features. I thought she had grown prettier than ever, and no doubt my looks told her as much. We spent an hour in talking about Grenoble and her old friends, whom she gladly recalled to her memory, and then she went to fetch a young girl who was boarding at the convent, whom she liked and wanted to present to her aunt.

I seized the opportunity of telling Madame Morin that I was astonished at the likeness, that her very voice was like that of my Venetian M—— M——, and I begged her to obtain me the privilege of breakfasting with her niece the next day, and of presenting her with a dozen pounds of capital chocolate. I had brought it with me from Genoa.

"You must make her the present yourself," said Madame Morin, "for though she's a nun she's a woman, and we women much prefer a present from a man's than from a woman's hand."

M—— M—— returned with the superior of the convent, two other nuns, and the young boarder, who came from Lyons, and was exquisitely beautiful. I was obliged to talk to all the nuns, and Madame Morin told her niece that I wanted her to try some excellent chocolate I had brought from Genoa, but that I hoped her lay-sister would make it.

"Sir," said M—— M——, "kindly send me the chocolate, and to-morrow we will breakfast together with these dear sisters."

As soon as I got back to my inn I sent the chocolate with a respectful note, and I took supper in Madame Morin's room with her daughter and Mdlle. Desarmoises, of whom I was feeling more and more amorous, but I talked of M—— M—— all the time, and I could see that the aunt suspected that the pretty nun was not altogether a stranger to me.

I breakfasted at the convent and I remember that the chocolate, the biscuits, and the sweetmeats were served with a nicety which savoured somewhat of the world. When we had finished breakfast I told M—— M—— that she would not find it so easy to give me a dinner, with twelve persons sitting down to table, but I added that half the company could be in the convent and half in the parlour, separated from the convent by a light grating.

"It's a sight I should like to see," said I, "if you will allow me to pay all expenses."

"Certainly," replied M—— M——, and this dinner was fixed for the next day.

M—— M—— took charge of the whole thing, and promised to ask six nuns. Madame Morin, who knew my tastes, told her to spare nothing, and I warned her that I would send in the necessary wines.

I escorted Madame Morin, her daughter, and Mdlle. Desarmoises back to the hotel, and I then called on M. Magnan, to whom I had been recommended by the Chevalier Raiberti. I asked him to get me some of the best wine, and he took me down to his cellar, and told me to take what I liked. His wines proved to be admirable.

This M. Magnan was a clever man, of a pleasant appearance, and very comfortably off. He occupied an extremely large and convenient house outside the town, and there his agreeable wife dispensed hospitality. She had ten children, amongst whom there were four pretty daughters; the eldest, who was nineteen, was especially good-looking.

We went to the convent at eleven o'clock, and after an hour's conversation we were told that dinner was ready. The table was beautifully laid, covered with a fair white cloth, and adorned with vases filled with artificial flowers so strongly scented that the air of the parlour was quite balmy. The fatal grill was heavier than I had hoped. I found myself seated to the left of M—— M——, and totally unable to see her. The fair Desarmoises was at my right, and she entertained us all the time with her amusing stories.

We in the parlour were waited on by Le Duc and Costa, and the nuns were served by their lay-sisters. The abundant provision, the excellent wines, the pleasant though sometimes equivocal conversation, kept us all merrily employed for three hours. Mirth had the mastery over reason, or, to speak more plainly, we were all drunk; and if it had not been for the fatal grill, I could have had the whole eleven ladies without much trouble. The young Desarmoises was so gay, indeed, that if I had not restrained her she would probably have scandalised all the nuns, who would have liked nothing better. I was longing to have her to myself, that I might quench the flame she had kindled in my breast, and I had no doubt of my success on the first attempt. After coffee had been served, we went into another parlour and stayed there till night came on. Madame Morin took leave of her niece, and the hand-shakings, thanks, and promises of remembrance between me and the nuns, lasted for a good quarter of an hour. After I had said aloud to M—— M—— that I hoped to have the pleasure of seeing her before I left, we went back to the inn in high good humour with our curious party which I still remember with pleasure.

Madame Morin gave me a letter for her cousin Madame Varnier, and I promised to write to her from Paris, and tell her all about the fair Mdlle. Roman. I presented the daughter with a beautiful pair of ear-rings, and I gave Madame Morin twelve pounds of good chocolate which M. Magnan got me, and which the lady thought had come from Genoa. She went off at eight o'clock preceded by Le Duc, who had orders to greet the doorkeeper's family on my behalf.

At Magnan's I had a dinner worthy of Lucullus, and I promised to stay with him whenever I passed Chamberi, which promise I have faithfully performed.

On leaving the gourmand's I went to the convent, and M—— M—— came down alone to the grating. She thanked me for coming to see her, and added that I had come to disturb her peace of mind.

"I am quite ready, dearest, to climb the harden wall, and I shall do it more dexterously than your wretched humpback."

"Alas! that may not be, for, trust me, you are already spied upon. Everybody here is sure that we knew each other at Aix. Let us forget all, and thus spare ourselves the torments of vain desires."

"Give me your hand."

"No. All is over. I love you still, probably I shall always love you; but I long for you to go, and by doing so, you will give me a proof of your love."

"This is dreadful; you astonish me. You appear to me in perfect health, you are prettier than ever, you are made for the worship of the sweetest of the gods, and I can't understand how, with a temperament like yours, you can live in continual abstinence."

"Alas! lacking the reality we console ourselves by pretending. I will not conceal from you that I love my young boarder. It is an innocent passion, and keeps my mind calm. Her caresses quench the flame which would otherwise kill me."

"And that is not against your conscience?"

"I do not feel any distress on the subject."

"But you know it is a sin."

"Yes, so I confess it."

"And what does the confessor say?"

"Nothing. He absolves me, and I am quite content."

"And does the pretty boarder confess, too?"

"Certainly, but she does not tell the father of a matter which she thinks is no sin."

"I wonder the confessor has not taught her, for that kind of instruction is a great pleasure."

"Our confessor is a wise old man."

"Am I to leave you, then, without a single kiss?"

"Not one."

"May I come again to-morrow? I must go the day after."

"You may come, but I cannot see you by myself as the nuns might talk. I will bring my little one with me to save appearances. Come after dinner, but into the other parlour."

If I had not known M—— M—— at Aix, her religious ideas would have astonished me; but such was her character. She loved God, and did not believe that the kind Father who made us with passions would be too severe because we had not the strength to subdue them. I returned to the inn, feeling vexed that the pretty nun would have no more to do with me, but sure of consolation from the fair Desarmoises.

I found her sitting on her lover's bed; his poor diet and the fever had left him in a state of great weakness. She told me that she would sup in my room to leave him in quiet, and the worthy young man shook my hand in token of his gratitude.

As I had a good dinner at Magnan's I ate very little supper, but my companion who had only had a light meal ate and drank to an amazing extent. I gazed at her in a kind of wonder, and she enjoyed my astonishment. When my servants had left the room I challenged her to drink a bowl of punch with me, and this put her into a mood which asked for nothing but laughter, and which laughed to find itself deprived of reasoning power. Nevertheless, I cannot accuse myself of taking an advantage of her condition, for in her voluptuous excitement she entered eagerly into the pleasure to which I excited her till two o'clock in the morning. By the time we separated we were both of us exhausted.

I slept till eleven, and when I went to wish her good day I found her smiling and as fresh as a rose. I asked her how she had passed the rest of the night.

"Very pleasantly," said she, "like the beginning of the night."

"What time would you like to have dinner?"

"I won't dine; I prefer to keep my appetite for supper."

Here her lover joined in, saying in a weak voice,—

"It is impossible to keep up with her."

"In eating or drinking?" I asked.

"In eating, drinking, and in other things," he replied, with a smile. She laughed, and kissed him affectionately.

This short dialogue convinced me that Mdlle. Desarmoises must adore her lover; for besides his being a handsome young man, his disposition was exactly suitable to hers. I dined by myself, and Le Duc came in as I was having dessert. He told me that the door-keeper's daughters and their pretty cousin had made him wait for them to write to me, and he gave me three letters and three dozen of gloves which they had presented me. The letters urged me to come and spend a month with them, and gave me to understand that I should be well pleased with my treatment. I had not the courage to return to a town, where with my reputation I should have been obliged to draw horoscopes for all the young ladies or to make enemies by refusing.

After I had read the letters from Grenoble I went to the convent and announced my presence, and then entered the parlour which M—— M—— had indicated. She soon came down with the pretty boarder, who feebly sustained my part in her amorous ecstacies. She had not yet completed her twelfth year, but she was extremely tall and well developed for her age. Gentleness, liveliness, candour, and wit were united in her features, and gave her expression an exquisite charm. She wore a well-made corset which disclosed a white throat, to which the fancy easily added the two spheres which would soon appear there. Her entrancing face, her raven locks, and her ivory throat indicated what might be concealed, and my vagrant imagination made her into a budding Venus. I began by telling her that she was very pretty, and would make her future husband a happy man. I knew she would blush at that. It may be cruel, but it is thus that the language of seduction always begins. A girl of her age who does not blush at the mention of marriage is either an idiot or already an expert in profligacy. In spite of this, however, the blush which mounts to a young girl's cheek at the approach of such ideas is a puzzling problem. Whence does it arise? It may be from pure simplicity, it may be from shame, and often from a mixture of both feelings. Then comes the fight between vice and virtue, and it is usually virtue which has to give in. The desires—the servants of vice—usually attain their ends. As I knew the young boarder from M—— M——'s description, I could not be ignorant of the source of those blushes which added a fresh attraction to her youthful charms.

Pretending not to notice anything, I talked to M—— M—— for a few moments, and then returned to the assault. She had regained her calm.

"What age are you, pretty one?" said I.

"I am thirteen."

"You are wrong," said M—— M——, "you have not yet completed your twelfth year."

"The time will come," said I, "when you will diminish the tale of your years instead of increasing it."

"I shall never tell a lie, sir; I am sure of that."

"So you want to be a nun, do you?"

"I have not yet received my vocation; but even if I live in the world I need not be a liar."

"You are wrong; you will begin to lie as soon as you have a lover."

"Will my lover tell lies, too?"

"Certainly he will."

"If the matter were really so, then, I should have a bad opinion of love; but I do not believe it, for I love my sweetheart here, and I never conceal the truth from her."

"Yes, but loving a man is a different thing to loving a woman."

"No, it isn't; it's just the same."

"Not so, for you do not go to bed with a woman and you do with your husband."

"That's no matter, my love would be the same."

"What? You would not rather sleep with me than with M—— M——?"

"No, indeed I should not, because you are a man and would see me."

"You don't want a man to see you, then?"

"No."

"Do you think you are so ugly, then?"

At this she turned to M—— M—— and said, with evident vexation, "I am not really ugly, am I?"

"No, darling," said M—— M——, bursting with laughter, "it is quite the other way; you are very pretty." With these words she took her on her knee and embraced her tenderly.

"Your corset is too tight; you can't possibly have such a small waist as that."

"You make a mistake, you can put your hand there and see for yourself."

"I can't believe it."

M—— M—— then held her close to the grill and told me to see for myself.

At the same moment she turned up her dress.

"You were right," said I, "and I owe you an apology;" but in my heart I cursed the grating and the chemise.

"My opinion is," said I to M—— M——, "that we have here a little boy."

I did not wait for a reply, but satisfied myself by my sense of touch as to her sex, and I could see that the little one and her governess were both pleased that my mind was at rest on the subject.

I drew my hand away, and the little girl looked at M—— M——, and reassured by her smiling air asked if she might go away for a moment. I must have reduced her to a state in which a moment's solitude was necessary, and I myself was in a very excited condition.

As soon as she was gone I said to M—— M——,

"Do you know that what you have shewn me has made me unhappy?"

"Has it? Why?"

"Because your boarder is charming, and I am longing to enjoy her."

"I am sorry for that, for you can't possibly go any further; and besides, I know you, and even if you could satisfy your passion without danger to her, I would not give her up to you, you would spoil her."

"How?"

"Do you think that after enjoying you she would care to enjoy me? I should lose too heavily by the comparison."

"Give me your hand."

"No."

"Stay, one moment."

"I don't want to see anything."

"Not a little bit?"

"Nothing at all."

"Are you angry with me, then?"

"Not at all. If you have been pleased I am glad, and if you have filled her with desires she will love me all the better."

"How pleasant it would be, sweetheart, if we could all three of us be together alone and at liberty!"

"Yes; but it is impossible."

"Are you sure that no inquisitive eye is looking upon us?"

"Quite sure."

"The height of that fatal grill has deprived me of the sight of many charms."

"Why didn't you go to the other parlour it is much lower there."

"Let us go there, then."

"Not to-day; I should not be able to give any reason for the change."

"I will come again to-morrow, and start for Lyons in the evening."

The little boarder came back, and I stood up facing her. I had a number of beautiful seals and trinkets hanging from my watch-chain, and I had not had the time to put myself in a state of perfect decency again.

She noticed it, and by way of pretext she asked if she might look at them.

"As long as you like; you may look at them and touch them as well."

M—— M—— foresaw what would happen and left the room, saying that she would soon be back. I had intended to deprive the young boarder of all interest in my seals by shewing her a curiosity of another kind. She did not conceal her pleasure in satisfying her inquisitiveness on an object which was quite new to her, and which she was able to examine minutely for the first time in her life. But soon an effusion changed her curiosity into surprise, and I did not interrupt her in her delighted gaze.

I saw M—— M—— coming back slowly, and I lowered my shirt again, and sat down. My watch and chains were still on the ledge of the grating, and M—— M—— asked her young friend if the trinkets had pleased her.

"Yes," she replied, but in a dreamy and melancholy voice. She had learnt so much in the course of less than two hours that she had plenty to think over. I spent the rest of the day in telling M—— M—— the adventures I had encountered since I had left her; but as I had not time to finish my tale I promised to return the next day at the same time.

The little girl, who had been listening to me all the time, though I appeared to be only addressing her friend, said that she longed to know the end of my adventure with the Duke of Matelone's mistress.

I supped with the fair Desarmoises, and after giving her sundry proofs of my affection till midnight, and telling her that I only stopped on for her sake, I went to bed.

The next day after dinner I returned to the convent, and having sent up my name to M—— M—— I entered the room where the grating was more convenient.

Before long M—— M—— arrived alone, but she anticipated my thoughts by telling me that her pretty friend would soon join her.

"You have fired her imagination. She has told me all about it, playing a thousand wanton tricks, and calling me her dear husband. You have seduced the girl, and I am very glad you are going or else you would drive her mad. You will see how she has dressed herself."

"Are you sure of her discretion?"

"Perfectly, but I hope you won't do anything in my presence. When I see the time coming I will leave the room."

"You are an angel, dearest, but you might be something better than that if you would—"

"I want nothing for myself; it is out of the question."

"You could—"

"No, I will have nothing to do with a pastime which would rekindle fires that are hardly yet quenched. I have spoken; I suffer, but let us say no more about it."

At this moment the young adept came in smiling, with her eyes full of fire. She was dressed in a short pelisse, open in front, and an embroidered muslin skirt which did not go beyond her knees. She looked like a sylph.

We had scarcely sat down when she reminded me of the place where my tale had stopped. I continued my recital, and when I was telling them how Donna Lucrezia shewed me Leonilda naked, M—— M—— went out, and the sly little puss asked me how I assured myself that my daughter was a maid.

I took hold of her through the fatal grating, against which she placed her pretty body, and shewed her how assured myself of the fact, and the girl liked it so much that she pressed my hand to the spot. She then gave me her hand that I might share her pleasure, and whilst this enjoyable occupation was in progress M—— M—— appeared. My sweetheart said hastily,—

"Never mind, I told her all about it. She is a good creature and will not be vexed." Accordingly M—— M—— pretended not to see anything, and the precocious little girl wiped her hand in a kind of voluptuous ecstacy, which shewed how well she was pleased.

I proceeded with my history, but when I came to the episode of the poor girl who was 'tied', describing all the trouble I had vainly taken with her, the little boarder got so curious that she placed herself in the most seducing attitude so that I might be able to shew her what I did. Seeing this M—— M—— made her escape.

"Kneel down on the ledge, and leave the rest to me," said the little wanton.

The reader will guess what she meant, and I have no doubt that she would have succeeded in her purpose if the fire which consumed me had not distilled itself away just at the happy moment.

The charming novice felt herself sprinkled, but after ascertaining that nothing more could be done she withdrew in some vexation. My fingers, however, consoled her for the disappointment, and I had the pleasure of seeing her look happy once more.

I left these charming creatures in the evening, promising to visit them again in a year, but as I walked home I could not help reflecting how often these asylums, supposed to be devoted to chastity and prayer, contain in themselves the hidden germs of corruption. How many a timorous and trustful mother is persuaded that the child of her affection will escape the dangers of the world by taking refuge in the cloister. But behind these bolts and bars desires grow to a frenzied extreme; they crave in vain to be satisfied.

When I returned to the inn I took leave of the wounded man, whom I was happy to see out of danger. In vain I urged him to make use of my purse; he told me, with an affectionate embrace, that he had sufficient money, and if not, he had only to write to his father. I promised to stop at Lyons, and to oblige Desarmoises to desist from any steps he might be taking against them, telling them I had a power over him which would compel him to obey. I kept my word. After we had kissed and said good-bye, I took his future bride into my room that we might sup together and enjoy ourselves till midnight; but she could not have been very pleased with my farewell salute, for I was only able to prove my love for her once, as M—— M——'s young friend had nearly exhausted me.

I started at day-break, and the next day I reached the "Hotel du Parc," at Lyons. I sent for Desarmoises, and told him plainly that his daughter's charms had seduced me, that I thought her lover worthy of her, and that I expected him out of friendship for me to consent to the marriage. I went further, and told him that if he did not consent to everything that very instant I could no longer be his friend, and at this he gave in. He executed the requisite document in the presence of two witnesses, and I sent it to Chamberi by an express messenger.

This false marquis made me dine with him in his poor house. There was nothing about his younger daughter to remind me of the elder, and his wife inspired me with pity. Before I left I managed to wrap up six Louis in a piece of paper, and gave it to her without the knowledge of her husband. A grateful look shewed me how welcome the present was.

I was obliged to go to Paris, so I gave Desarmoises sufficient money for him to go to Strasburg, and await me there in company with my Spaniard.

I thought myself wise in only taking Costa, but the inspiration came from my evil genius.

I took the Bourbonnais way, and on the third day I arrived at Paris, and lodged at the Hotel du St. Esprit, in the street of the same name.

Before going to bed I sent Costa with a note to Madame d'Urfe, promising to come and dine with her the next day. Costa was a good-looking young fellow, and as he spoke French badly and was rather a fool I felt sure that Madame d'Urfe would take him for some extraordinary being. She wrote to say that she was impatiently expecting me.

"How did the lady receive you, Costa?"

"She looked into a mirror, sir, and said some words I could make nothing of; then she went round the room three times burning incense; then she came up to me with a majestic air and looked me in the face; and at last she smiled very pleasantly, and told me to wait for a reply in the ante-chamber."

The End